W9-BRN-246

DATE			

CHINA DIARY

China Diary

Charlotte Y. Salisbury

introduction by
Harrison E. Salisbury

74-551

WALKER AND COMPANY
New York

For my children
   Charlotte, Ellen, Rosina, and Curtis

INTRODUCTION

The woman's eye. With all the talk about Women's Liberation, male chauvinism and equality of the sexes I think we have missed a point. There is a woman's eye and it is not a man's eye. It is different in degree and kind. It is as sensitive as a dragonfly's wing and as penetrating as a laser beam. It cuts through cant, ignores the superficial and effortlessly penetrates to the heart of the matter. Nor should this surprise us for both nature and society have combined to give woman an openness to sight and sound and sensation, a deftness of response, a clarity of feeling which in men is repressed and sublimated by environment and social factors. And this, I think, is why when we want to get the feel of a country, when we look for insight into a strange or complex people, when we want to understand the simple motivations that charismatic leaders so often conceal behind a mirror of glittering words and phrases we turn not to the labored analysis of a learned doctor but to the swift and certain intuition of a woman who looks on the world with clear, unclouded eyes and records her response with a warm and frank heart.

I have been traveling the back countries of the world for half my life or more—the Communist countries of Europe,

Russia, the lesser known regions of Asia, the emergent Communist states of the East—China, Mongolia and all the others. I know these countries, I have lived in them, worked in them, studied them, analyzed them. But it is not until recent years when Charlotte began to accompany me on my long missions to Asia, Russia and China that I began to get through her insight a third dimension in what had been up to that time a largely two-dimensional vision.

I think this insight is especially valuable in countries like China where the culture and philosophy (quite without regard for that associated with the Communist regime) is so alien to our own. The essence of China, to be sure, is the Chinese people and their way of life. Sometimes, a politically oriented observer like myself tends to forget this or to minimize it in a preoccupation with ideology, differences in Marxist systems and balance-of-power politics. But Charlotte's eye is on the people and even when they may be going through some ridiculous politically motivated routine such as the Dance of the Pig Breeders she does not forget that behind the baggy trousers and bulky tunics there are human beings with feelings, desires, aspirations and emotions that guide and modify their reactions to the government and party which dominate their lives.

When one wants to muse philosophically upon the nature of the American Republic and its impact upon Europe in the first half of the nineteenth century, De Tocqueville is the obvious answer. But when one wants to know what American society was like, what kind of people inhabited our continent, their manners, their mores, the color of their life, Harriet Martineau is the inevitable authority.

There is every likelihood that during the remaining part of this century—and probably for a long time thereafter—China is going to loom very large in our lives. I think she will loom larger and larger with the growth of her industry, the development of her political and social system, the strengthening of the Chinese state and the inevitable expansion of her population beyond the one billion mark. China will be a factor in every foreign policy decision of our future. In fact, she is already.

It is quite impossible for us to know too much about China and the Chinese. This is a nation and a people that have attracted the interest, curiosity and power hunger of western states for centuries. She has always been the great enigma. The mysterious east is a phrase that came into being to describe China. She still is. No one can read these pages, this day-by-day journey of discovery made by an alert and interested American woman from one end of China to another without feeling what a genuine discovery it really was to meet, live with, travel with, talk with, argue with Chinese people. Nor how intricately Chinese this vast country is, regardless of banners and symbols and slogans, or rulers and regimes and ideology.

China is not easy to understand. I do not pretend to understand it even after years of study, and certainly the six weeks' trip which Charlotte and I made to China in 1972 taught us to know our ignorance as much as it deepened our fund of knowledge. But this experience is in itself instructive because it teaches us once again what we are forever learning and forever forgetting—there are no quick answers to complex questions like China. The Chinese themselves, as Charlotte notes, help to reinforce this lesson because they say frankly and honestly that there are many things about their own country and particularly about the Cultural Revolution that they do not understand. If the Chinese themselves do not know the answers let us doubly beware of those non-Chinese who think they can sum up the whole situation with one ready cliché.

There are many ways of learning about a country but I

think the best way of all is through the people themselves. If we learn to know one Chinese or a few Chinese we can begin to understand at least some of the hundreds of millions of their brothers and sisters.

This is where I think a woman's heart and a woman's eye are best. Certainly that is true of Charlotte. Her feelings about people are solid and earthy. She senses what is real and what is diplomatic pretense. You can rely on her judgments.

The journey that Charlotte's diary records covered most of China—great cities like Peking, Shanghai, Hong Kong, Wuhan, Sian and Changsha; the north, northwest, center and south of China; the countryside as well as the cities; the farms as well as the factories; the schools, the hospitals, the children's facilities. We met high people like Premier Chou En-lai and Vice Chairman Soong Ching-ling (Mme. Sun Yat-sen) as well as simple peasants and housewives. Many things which were incomprehensible at the start of the trip gradually became clear with the passage of time, as Charlotte's diary records. But some, to be sure, are still mysteries. China may not be inscrutable but she still clings to her enigmas.

Many of us will be going to China as time goes by. I think everyone will find *China Diary* a useful guide as to what to expect; where it is interesting to go; what living is like; the nature of hotels and restaurants—as well as providing some key to the main facets of Chinese life. It is, in fact, a most useful handbook for travel in that country. And if it is not possible to make a personal journey you can see almost all of China come to life before your eyes on the pages of Charlotte's diary.

Harrison E. Salisbury
March, 1973

May 27

In the waiting room at Shumchumn,
the Chinese side of the border

RED FLAGS are blowing in the hot wind, loud music hits
my ears, swarms of young Chinese men and women stand at
posts or move slowly about, carrying bags, helping travelers
here and there, and I am walking across the covered railroad
bridge, doorway to the People's Republic of China, into this
country so mysterious and unknown to me, and to so many.
Three years ago at Macao we looked across a narrow creek at
the guard on the Chinese side and thought he looked fierce
and full of hate. The people I have seen so far, in the embassy in Ottawa where I picked up my visa, in the China
travel office in Hong Kong where I picked up my ticket, and
here, are calm, gentle, efficient, smiling and terribly friendly.

It is hard to believe I am really here, really in China. For
years Harrison has been trying to get in and since 1966 he
has done everything he could possibly think of, bombarded
people in and out of China with letters and wires, pestered

1

people who have even the slightest connection with China; every day he has tried to think of something new and effective to do. On that long trip around the borders of China in 1966, over forty thousand miles, he always hoped that in the next place he might be able to cross the border. But it never happened. And last year after the Ping-Pong exchange and three other members of the *New York Times* staff were admitted, still no word came for him. Now, at last, we are here, in the country about which I wrote only six years ago, ". . . the farthest land in the world from us." What will it be like? Will we react as most of the other visitors have, with enthusiasm and admiration for this country that in twenty short years has transformed itself, its government, society, and some say, even its people, in a complete rebirth?

Harrison must be in Peking now, back from his two-week trip to North Korea. It has been so strange not to be able to communicate with him. On May 4 he called me from Tokyo and said, "We have visas for China, meet me in Peking in three weeks." I had a letter mailed from Peking but I haven't been able to get in touch with him in any way, and since he's been in Pyongyang my only news of him has been through his stories in the paper. It reminds me of when he went to Hanoi in December 1966 and I didn't know anything about him until Christmas morning when headlines all over the world read, "U. S. Newsman in Hanoi." Thank God he isn't there now, especially with the terrible escalation of bombing that Nixon recently ordered.

I left Hong Kong this morning at eight, took the ferry to Kowloon and the train to Lo Wu, the British side of this border. I was shocked at the banks of the inlets along the way, littered with trash, garbage, cans, papers, and except for the mountains and water at first, the scenery is not either especially interesting or uninteresting. At Lo Wu my suitcase was carried for me across the bridge, I filled out a typical custom form stating whether I had watches, jewelry, gold, radio, tape recorder, guns, etc., and stood by my bags at the inspection counter. A shy young soldier looked at the form, asked me what I had in my bags. I answered only personal clothing. He smiled and said in perfect English, "The inspection is over."

This big building where I am waiting is just across the border, has several waiting rooms, all airy and filled with chairs and sofas slip-covered in fresh light cotton. Lace antimacassars are on the backs and arms of all the furniture. The swarms of Chinese, men and women, wear the same kind of clothes, loose baggy pants and either a shirt hanging outside or a jacket. Soldiers wear khaki, others are in blue or gray. About twenty-five other people are waiting too, some Canadians, Ambassador Valdez of Peru, his wife and daughter, no Americans except me. I had lunch with the ambassador's family—we had introduced ourselves on the train—a delicious lunch that was given to us and served by a cheerful girl with pigtails in a big white dining room with round tables, each covered with an embroidered cloth. I can't get over the general attitude of courtesy that I feel, and felt immediately; we don't encounter such good manners at home. Never have I seen such polite, civilized people, friendly and so attractive, and if the comparison of the ladies room in the Hong Kong station with the one in this building is typical of all comparisons, there can be no doubt about the better system. In the former a filthy attendant was picking her feet in a basin, three holes in the floor were filled with blood and feces not flushed away and flies buzzed around the mess— smelly and disgusting; here there is a regular toilet in an airy room, clean and spotless.

On the plane to Peking

Everyone has reported how clean and neat the Chinese

3

trains are, but it is not easy to imagine until you see one. Freshly painted and washed on the outside, inside it is almost like a living room, or maybe your grandmother's summer porch. The seats have cotton covers and lace antimacassars; they are arranged so that four face each other, and there is a table between them. Cups, which were soon filled with tea by the girl porter, stood on each table. As soon as she had passed out the tea she mopped the floor. Not a speck of dust or dirt anywhere, nor any bugs. Revolving fans on the ceiling kept us comfortable in spite of the heat as we passed through incredibly beautiful rice fields and farmlands, simple and marvelous scenes of men and women working, water buffalos, not a sight of a machine of any kind, all pastoral and old and somehow elegant and timeless. I sat with the Valdez'. I had suggested to them that they might like to sit just with their own family, but they replied in unison, "You are part of our family here." They have been in China a few months and are full of enthusiasm for what they have seen. They feel that the Chinese really have created a new man, a man who knows what he wants and is peaceful and kind. (A Canadian waiting at the airport told me the same thing, that people here really are thoughtful of their fellowman and help him, they care about each other; they are taught and trained to be like this in kindergarten.)

At Canton I was met by Mr. Soong who was charming and friendly. He had been with Harrison and John Lee, Tokyo Bureau Chief of the *New York Times*, when they first came in on their way to North Korea. Everything is terribly efficient. I didn't have to carry my bag; I had some money problems because I didn't realize I needed so much more than I had with me—I thought mistakenly I had paid for my ticket through to Peking—but these were quickly and pleasantly solved. We waited about three hours in the airport, which is like any airport that can get by with only one

4

big waiting room except that a girl with a wagon carrying thermos jugs of hot water served tea gratis to anyone who wanted it before boarding the plane. The stewardesses are serious young girls with braids and clothes just like the men; blue pants, white shirts and khaki jackets; all baggy. They walk up and down the aisle making sure everything is o.k. and I feel it must be with such guardians—it can't be anything else. One has just passed the candy for landing and, seeing I was writing, turned on my light. There is a dignity about each person that I have seen, a self-respect that is very evident.

At the Chien Men Hotel, 12:30 A.M.

Harrison is not here, which certainly is disappointing, and no word of or from him. I only hope that he is all right. He wrote that he'd be here yesterday. Well, I have a huge room reminiscent of the National Hotel in Moscow. Everyone is very nice and I can call the Valdez' if I need anything. Sort of a flop, though, after so much looking forward.

May 28

9:30 A.M.

SLEPT WELL, the bed is marvelously comfortable. Wakened early by the usual rapid-fire noises of every place I've ever been in Asia, bicycle bells, horns honking, children playing, even at quarter of seven. A dull gray day and I really do feel terribly anticlimatic. Mrs. Fan, a tiny Chinese woman from the travel bureau who met me last night, said I should stay in the hotel all day in case there is news of H., and there's no place to go anyway. Last night when we passed the Peking Hotel, where the Valdez' live, I asked if this hotel were near it, and Mrs. Fan said, "Oh yes, not far," and then we drove for at least fifteen minutes until we got here, far for walking, surely. Well, I'll plan a schedule as if I were in school, one hour for writing, two for reading, and so on. I had a nice breakfast, had coffee earlier as there is a huge thermos of hot water in my room at all times and I see them in the hall outside many doors. What a wonderful idea; no ringing for tea or coffee and waiting for hours, or trying to

6

make it oneself and burning out those electric coils.

This morning I saw such bustling and cleaning. In the dining room men and girls were scrubbing walls, windows, tops of screens, everything—standing on tables piled two and three on top of another so they could reach the top. There seem to be hundreds of people on this floor who work in the hotel.

Later: Just as I had written the above and had gone to the hall desk to get some tea, the telephone rang and Mrs. Fan announced, "Your husband is arriving in one hour in a special plane." No time for her to come here, I must get a taxi and pick her up at her office and we'd go to the airport. She would call the desk and tell them. So off we went and at one thirty there was Harrison stepping out of his special plane and looking wonderful. Nothing more to say except that it is heavenly after so long. We have been catching up with news. He didn't even know that Tony Lewis, columnist of the *New York Times,* was in Hanoi. The only awful thing is I can't remember anything that's been on the "Op Ed" page, of which H. is editor, except two articles I didn't like. Tomorrow I guess our trip will begin in earnest as we go to the Foreign Office at 9:00 A.M.

May 29

Noon

AFTER SLEEPING all through the night, which I haven't done for many nights, we went to see Mr. Ma at the Foreign Office to discuss our visit, what we want to do, whom we want to see and talk to, where we want to go. Our interpreter, Mr. Yao Wei, accompanied us, though Mr. Ma speaks perfect English. H. wants to go to Inner Mongolia and Sinkiang and I would rather go to Tibet than almost anything in the world, but they can't be visited yet—the Cultural Revolution is still going on in these places. I wonder what that really means: I suppose that things are not under control yet, not in order. It is interesting that this "new man," peaceful and full of good will, is a product of such upheaval, but I guess that is what revolution means. I wonder if we will ever understand the Cultural Revolution, know what happened, know how a lot of people honestly felt, and feel now.

I am so aware of the difference here in the atmosphere, feeling and look of the people, the general attitude, compared to Russia I can't get over it. Perhaps one day isn't much to go on, but the people in the hotel, the travel people, Mr. Ma, our interpreter, anyone we have seen so far, are very different. Mr. Ma looks and has mannerisms very much like people I have met in Sikkim, the tiny country on Tibet's southern border. He reminds me especially of the Chogyal, or King, and the similarities are natural for Sikkim's royal family came originally from Tibet and many Chinese have the same broad handsome faces.

9:30 P.M.

This afternoon Harrison worked at his typewriter and I went with John Lee to the Temple of Heaven, an area nearly four miles long, where sacrifices were made in hopes of a good harvest and where the emperors paid homage to the gods, talked to them and told them what had been going on. The big temple, or Hall of Prayer for Good Harvests, is three-tiered, round, very colorful, brightly painted, something like the temples in Sikkim and Mongolia and, I imagine, Tibet, but on a much grander scale and far more beautiful. The Imperial Heavenly Vault and the Round Mound with three tiers of marble and stone-carved balustrades are the other two main buildings. Wonderful walls and gates surround it all. These buildings were originally built in the fifteenth century and it is very exciting to see some of the past in the middle of today's Peking, which from the little I've seen seems drab and dull with hardly any color but gray.

May 30

4:30 P.M.

JUST BACK FROM the Great Wall and the Ming Tombs with Mr. Ma and Yao Wei and John Lee. We started at 8:30 A.M. in two cars, Mr. Ma with us and Yao Wei and John following, on a long drive through flat farmland with a factory here and there. These are communes with factories related to their needs, farm machinery, chemical fertilizers, cotton yard goods; brick kilns, things they use and should know how to make—to be "self-sufficient," the motto we have already heard many times in two days. The land is really a plain; hot, dry, dusty, and ringed by those marvelous jagged Chinese mountains, looking just as they do in old paintings, one layer behind another in the mist (or is it dust from the Gobi desert or smog from the commune factories?). Many trees have been planted and a big dam near the tombs supplies water for irrigation as well as electric power. Many people are in the fields, many on the road on foot, bicycles, and trucks and buses. Many have carts, usually pulled by three animals, the anchor animal, as it is called, in the middle between shafts, and one or two others, sometimes three more, harnessed at the side or ahead. The carts are full of wood, coal, manure, vegetables, anything you can think of, and they are heavy. About one hour out of Peking we saw much industry and plenty of smokestacks belching out thick, black smoke. I thought of what I had been told in Ottawa, that no factory was allowed to start operating unless the problems created by waste materials and smoke had been solved.

The Great Wall is not such a surprise to see at first—it is gray and doesn't look especially impressive; but when you are on it and see that it is eighteen feet wide across the top so that several horses could gallop along it abreast, and that it goes almost straight up in some places, terribly steep, and when you finally make it up to the highest tower and as far as you can see in both directions this stone snake winds, for more than three thousand miles, then you begin to realize how fantastic it is. And especially when we know it has been in existence in one form or another since around the fifth century B.C. At different times in history the Great Wall has been an important defense, at others it was abandoned as such, and at one period it was in the middle of a state, so not necessary to anyone. Now it has been rebuilt in several areas as a tourist attraction. There were many Chinese on a day off, all looking cheerful and healthy, but dull as far as their clothes go. Our companion Mr. Ma was very smart in his well-fitting jacket, not drab at all though it was the same kind of jacket everyone else wears.

I am relieved to know that the Great Wall is being kept as a historic monument as are the Temple of Heaven and the Forbidden City. I had imagined from the stories we heard during the Cultural Revolution of the Red Guards storming museums and private collections and universities, throwing

11

out books, dashing Ming vases in the gutter, destroying objects representing bourgeois reactionary society with no thought of their value in the overall history of China, that not only would nothing be left, but that the attitude of the government would be to get rid of all the past and its creations. Obviously this is not true.

Our Chinese companions told us about President Nixon visiting the Great Wall and Harrison asked, "What did he say?" Laughing, they said he replied, "It's a great wall." They thought that was awfully funny.

Lunch was a picnic (they had brought a box for each of us) in a guest house, delicious sandwiches, cold chicken, the kind H. likes, brown and tough and tasty—he will not eat chicken at home because he says it is full of chemicals and hormones, and from the beginning the chicken is subjected to such an unnatural life that it is bound to be unhealthy, besides having no taste or feel. It's true, of course, but it makes it hard to feed him; chicken is always available and generally cheaper than most meats, and I am so accustomed to our anemic food that I even like it and I don't like Asian chicken. Fruit and orange soda, beer and tea made up the rest of our lunch. Conversation was easy—our hosts are more interested in what Harrison knows about Russia than they are in any other subject we could talk about, and they kept up a lively questioning.

After lunch we went to the Ming tombs. In the past Chinese kings and emperors planned and built their tombs near their capital and during their lives. These were planned with great care, special attention being given to the site to be sure that all evil influences were avoided. The Ming site was chosen by the third emperor in the early fifteenth century and all the succeeding Ming emperors but one are buried here with their empresses and second wives. It is a large area of about six square miles. The hills to the north form a semicircular backdrop and protection against wind and dust storms, a river runs through the plain and in those days the forests stretched out from the tombs to cover the mountains. No one was allowed to enter this area except the caretakers, whose jobs were inherited, and the emperor, when he went to pay his respects to his ancestors or to oversee the work. Even he got off his horse and walked from the gate, for to be on horseback was not allowed, nor was cultivation of any kind, wood cutting or removing stones. The whole area was surrounded by a red wall in the valley and lookout posts in the hills, but nothing remains now except the stone portico and red gate and part of a pavilion beyond the gate. The red gate has three large archways which used to have great wooden doors and only the dead emperor's body was taken through the center door; the living emperors used the side doors. The Sacred Way, or The Way of the Spirit, the nearly four-mile-long avenue of stone animals, leads from the portico to the gate of the chief tomb.

We drove through the red gate and got out to walk between those statues whose many pictures we have all seen: lions, camels, elephants, horses, one of each standing and one kneeling; other mythical creatures with hooves and horns, twenty-four in all. After these come twelve statues of emperors and mandarins in elaborate clothes or military attire. These statues are of the fifteenth century, the time of the first tomb, and the meaning is probably that they were the animals who served the dead in the next world. This sacred way now goes over a modern bridge from which you can see the new dam, built in 1958. Chairman Mao and leading members of the Communist Party worked on this project and it was finished in six months. It provides irrigation in the plains as well as electric power.

We saw the Ding ling tomb, the tomb of Emperor Wan Li and his two wives, who lived in the sixteenth and early sev-

13

enteenth centuries. This was the first tomb to be excavated by a scientific and governmental group in 1956, and the work continued until 1958. You approach the entrance to the tomb through courtyards and terraces and, though most of the original buildings have disappeared, at the end of the third courtyard the Square Tower stands, looking as permanent as China herself. Massive and built of brick, it has survived the fires and destruction of the other buildings. Steps on each side lead to the top and you can get a good look at the country and area of the tombs.

I am familiar with small Etruscan tombs in Italy and I have seen pictures, diagrams and models of Egyptian tombs, but I wasn't prepared for the size and extent of this. A wide passage leads to the stairs, which are new, have several landings and seem to go down into the very center of the earth. A long, high-vaulted central corridor containing three altars leads to the main chamber where the coffins were found along with twenty-six chests filled with precious objects. Two other chambers, one on each side of the corridor, each with a dais for a coffin, were found empty. The objects from the main chamber are now in the museum rooms in the third courtyard and they are as beautiful as anything I have ever seen. Gold utensils and bowls, porcelain vases and dishes, elaborate headdresses of jewels and feathers, material and clothes, swords, all the things that were used by the emperor and his family and household. Some are original but some are copies because the originals were in such bad shape. It is encouraging to realize that in spite of the lack of beauty in contemporary Chinese life, they have not forgotten their famous artistic skills.

We didn't go to any more tombs as not many have been excavated, and those that have been were closed, but we walked through the gate and buildings of the Chang ling tomb. The vastness and scale of the halls is staggering. The

Hall of Eminent Favors stands on three terraces of white marble with balustrades and steps and a central ramp magnificently carved with dragons. These ramps, with steps on either side, were for the emperor's sedan chair, and the porters used the steps while the chair must have seemed to slide down this beautiful ramp. In front of it are four large porcelain stoves that were used for burning offerings. The hall is 220 feet long and 105 feet wide and has thirty-two enormous pillars made of whole trees three feet thick holding up the yellow tiled roof. Twenty-eight slightly smaller columns, two feet six inches through, help to support the horizontal beams and the lower roof. The few inner pillars are painted gold, the rest bright red. The paneled ceiling is painted in squares of green, white and red.

We got back just in time to change and go out to dinner at the most famous Peking-duck restaurant in Peking. Our host was the head of the Information Service, a very sharp, shrewd man; guests included a newspaperman and his wife who had lived in London for four years, another woman and two men from the Information Service. We had about twenty-five dishes of duck, starting with something made from the webs of the feet and going through all the insides and liver, the latter crisp and airy and delicious, then roast duck, which we wrapped up in very thin pancakes with tiny scallions. Next we wrapped slices of duck in a split wheat bun, but I skipped that and am now sorry as I don't know what it tasted like. But I was just too full. Two kinds of duck soup were served and dessert was cut-up fruit, which smelled and tasted more like perfume than fruit. A Chinese lady said to me, "It takes strategy to get through a Chinese dinner," making a play on the title of one of the new operas, "Taking Tiger Mountain by Strategy." I must learn that strategy if I am to survive the dinners we are bound to go to. No one urged us to eat the way we have always heard they did in the past, but everything is so good I hate to miss any of it. The food we get in even the best Chinese restaurants in New York will now seem like mush.

The talk was mostly about the Soviet Union, which the Chinese seem to be preoccupied with these days. They pump Harrison every chance they get and of course, he loves it. I am amazed that the men we have talked to are so well informed about the United States; they have read every current book about what prominent people in our country are thinking about China, Russia, the world, but most of all, they have read everything about Vietnam. The horror of the war is much closer here than anywhere else we've been since that long trip in Asia in 1966. So far, every conversation has begun with references to Vietnam; the bombing, the casualties and damage, the peace talks or lack of them. It is awful the way it makes us feel, so responsible and yet so helpless; it is like being ashamed of your parents when you're young and can't think of anything to say to defend them, only this is worse.

At one point, when H. said that everyone in New York had thought it was such a nice gesture for the Chinese to give a party for the Roosevelt Hotel staff and the New York policemen who had been their guards while there, our host said politely but firmly, "We don't regard people as inferior because they are waiters or policemen." He said it as if it were an unarguable point, that Americans do consider some people inferior, that we are snobby about jobs, think about status. There is no point in trying to explain that we don't; the fact that we don't usually give parties for hotel staffs and policemen is proof to the Chinese that we do feel superior, we do have this class consciousness.

The women at our dinner were lovely, friendly, interesting, and had complete equality with the men, but I don't see how they can stand looking so dreary. I don't know

16

which I mind the most, the bagginess and lack of shape of their clothes or the lack of color—the grays and blues are so drab. It is depressing. Even simple clothes can be becoming and attractive. I think people should look as nice as they can, and while I am horrified to learn from a man here that the money spent on cosmetics in the United States each year far exceeds the income of all the countries in Africa combined, still it would be nice to see these quite remarkable-looking women spruced up a bit.

May 31

THIS MORNING we drove out to a People's Commune about forty-five minutes from Peking. Communes were established during The Great Leap Forward. Beginning in 1958 this was a huge countrywide effort by the Chinese to pull themselves up by their bootstraps, so to speak, to a high rate of industrial and agricultural growth; factories were installed in the countryside and the People's Communes formed. Today more than seventy thousand communes exist, each containing five, ten, or more thousand people, depending on the area. This period also coincided with the disagreements between the governments of China and Russia, which ended in Russia pulling out all its advisers and workers in 1960. The Soviet Union didn't approve of the Chinese ideology and theories, didn't believe they would work along their own communist line. The Russians' leaving, bag and baggage, also made necessary the "innovations" we hear mentioned so often; somehow the Chinese had to "make do" with the unfinished factories and machinery.

Of course most Americans have heard a lot about life in the Chinese communes, of how men and women are divided, each in their commune, that there is no family life, no life between the sexes except working together in the fields and factories and studying the little red book. From what we saw today all of that is wrong. In reality, the Chinese commune is a series of villages or small communities. Especially in the real countryside, families live in their own one-story traditional peasant houses with a yard in front, a pen for a pig and a place to keep chickens, which run free in the daytime. These houses are clustered together, surrounded by fields of vegetables and rice paddies and orchards. In most communes near the cities apartment houses of three and four stories have been built and families pay very low rent for two or three rooms with toilet, sink, sometimes a shower, and kitchen. All communes are divided into workable units, which are broken down into production brigades and work teams with leaders responsible for getting the work parceled out and done.

Our principal host was a member of the administration of the commune, forty-eight years old, friendly and open, utterly disarming. All through our visit he kept saying we must feel free to find fault with anything we thought was not as it should be and, we, quite honestly, kept repeating that first of all we couldn't imagine doing such a thing and second, we couldn't see anything to find fault with. We visited two families, one with four generations all living together, the other with three; saw the hog farm, the dairy, stock farm, duck farm, a village shop, orchard, dispensary, flour mill, and had a perfectly delicious lunch. At the beginning and end of our visit we sat at a long table, drank tea and talked frankly with the administrator and several other members of the management, all of whom have something to do with

19

the Revolutionary Committee.

Both of the families we visited live in their own houses, which are the traditional one-story peasant houses of three rooms. Usually in these houses the beds are *kangs*, big, built-in platforms of stone or brick. In cold weather these are heated by smoke from the cooking stove, which circulates under the *kang*, as if the space were a huge oven, before going out a chimney or smokestack. Our interpreter, who realizes how much we think about pollution and waste disposal, said it is a good solution to those problems as the smoke has thinned out a lot by the time it gets outdoors. In summer they cook on another stove, nearer the door. A straw mat covers the *kang* and several quilts are rolled up at one end, one for each member of the family who sleeps there. There were five quilts on the big *kang* we saw first, for all the family except the younger couple and the baby, who slept in another room.

It is hard to see how they can have much, if any, privacy, and hard to imagine how a man and wife can sleep together in any intimacy with someone else in bed. Of course in the past almost everybody except kings and queens slept all together in beds to keep warm, and even now this kind of communal sleeping is not peculiar to China. I remember in the country at home several years ago a doctor in the village was summoned to help a woman in childbirth, and when he arrived at the house he found a baby had been born to the mother in a bed where two more children were sleeping, and they hadn't even waked up. In the newer apartment buildings the beds are the same as ours, double for the parents and bunk beds for children. Generally the parents sleep in a separate room; grandparents sleep with children.

The family of four generations has eight members, husband twenty-six, wife twenty-four, mother-in-law fifty-four, father-in-law fifty-six, grandmother seventy-eight, two younger sisters of the husband, and a baby. Four members of this family are in the commune work force, the young husband and wife, the father-in-law and one of the younger sisters; the other sister is still in school and the mother-in-law and the grandmother, who is actually a great grandmother, stay at home and take care of the house and the baby. The family's combined income is 1,300 yuan a year of which they get 600 in cash (a yuan is approximately forty cents so this is roughly $520 total and $240 in cash.) They receive their share of grain and vegetables from the commune and in addition they have their own hogs, chickens and eggs. Generally the hogs are sold and the family buys meat but sometimes they are slaughtered to celebrate Chinese New Year. The young wife was given time off from work to meet us and be our hostess; the older women were fussing over the baby and getting tea. Everywhere we have been we have been given tea; huge thermos jugs of boiled hot water are in every hotel room, house, office, airport, station, and even in this terrific heat the weak green tea is very refreshing. The young couple each has had nine years of schooling; they both graduated from what they call the middle school, equivalent to our junior high school. She will nurse her baby for about two years and has time out from whatever work she is doing in the field or in one of the factories, generally an hour twice during the work period.

We talked a little about the rights and place of women all over the world and she said, with feeling, that young Chinese women now have rights equal not only with men, but also with mothers-in-law. Traditionally, in all levels of Chinese society, the mother-in-law ran the family. A bride moved into her mother-in-law's house and did as she was told; she had no standing or authority until she became a mother-in-law herself. I was interested to hear this girl speak with such passion, but I guess a system so entrenched dies

21

hard in spite of governmental orders, and perhaps she still has to fight for her rights.

This family has a foot pedal sewing machine and the older women sew clothes and quilt covers and other household items, but the younger one doesn't have much time for sewing. We also talked about how many children she wanted—no more, only the baby she has. She uses pills given out by the dispensary; abortion is available to everyone simply on request and the same methods of birth control are used here as are all over the world—the pill, the IUD, diaphragms and condums. Men and women can also have operations to make them sterile, but these are not very popular.

The second family lived in the same kind of house and included a man and his wife in their late twenties, both of whom work in factories at the moment, three small children and the grandmother who works in one of the commune's nurseries and takes care of the baby there. The other children go to the kindergarten every day. This young wife says she doesn't want any more babies, but hers are very close and it doesn't seem as if she had taken advantage of the birth control that is supposed to be available. This family's income is 800 yuan a year, 300 of it in cash, about $320 total and $120 in cash. This may seem very little to us, but when you consider that in 1949 at the time of Liberation, over 90 percent of the Chinese people were illiterate and at any given moment at least half was below subsistence level— lived so close to the starvation line that any little thing would send them over—the present state of security represents a miracle. This family has its own plot for vegetables in the commune fields, its own hog and chickens, and they have planted more vegetables in the tiny space outside the house. They also have a radio and a sewing machine. One thing that surprised me is that there are no flowers anywhere, not even a few blossoms around a house, but I guess

it's because no one can afford the luxury of growing anything simply to look at, not to eat or use in some fashion.

The head of the hog farm is a girl, short, rather pretty
with tiny little hands. She proudly showed us around the
pens full of hogs of all sizes from tiny shoats to porkers on
their way to market. Everything is sold to the government
and meat is bought back for the commune. The head of the
dairy is a man, the cows are huge Holsteins and in the cow
barn a girl was milking by hand, "to learn how," not that it
is the most efficient way; generally they use machines. The
cows were in a regular barn with stanchions down each side,
clean and swept; the milk room was spotless, the milk is only
cooled here and stored until it is taken to a processing plant
in the city. The Chinese don't drink milk the way we do; in
fact most of it is dried to be used for children, a certain
amount is sent to hotels and some is used to make butter for
the hotels, too, as the Chinese don't use butter. They cook in
oil, either vegetable oil or, increasingly, in lard. I think that
lard is bad for them and I am sure the food won't be as good
or as delicate and nonfilling.

At noon we returned to our first meeting-room for lunch.
We washed our hands in basins of water that had been
placed on tables outside the door and went back in for some
more tea. After relaxing over a cup for a few minutes, we
moved to a round table that had been set up in the same
room with the group who had been with us everywhere we
had been so far. At home in a Chinese restaurant you drink
tea all through the meal; here we drink tea all day and
before and after meals, but we drink orange soda or beer
with ordinary meals, wine and *mao tai,* (the drink I call
white fire, it is about 160 proof) in tiny glasses, along with
soda and beer and mineral water at banquets. Also in restaurants at home we are served chop suey and here in China
there is no such thing; a Cantonese dish has a slight similari-

23

ty to what we call chow mein, but to a Chinese I believe it would be mush.

Dish after dish was brought in, each one accompanied by apologies that this was all they had, they wished it was better, etc. etc. If I had produced a single concoction as delectable as these I wouldn't have dreamed of apologizing. Each one was delicious, hot and tasty and light: fried eggplant in tiny bite-size pieces the way everything is here; eggs in several forms, scrambled, hard-boiled, in egg-drop soup; hot roasted peanuts, pork in heavenly sauce, wonderful beans, tender young cauliflower and lots of rice. Two bowls of rice at each meal is normal and I can't understand why we don't see many fat people. As a matter of fact, I had thought that there were no fat Chinese but that is not true; some of the girls who drive taxis from our hotel are plump, and often on the street you see older women who are round and comfortable looking. But obesity is not common, certainly not compared to America where it seems more than half the population is overweight, and most of the Chinese men are thin and spare and wiry. Everything we had for lunch was grown here at this commune. After we had finished, a girl brought each of us a hot wet cloth to wipe our hands and mouth, as is the custom regardless of where we are or whom we are with.

The famous Peking duck are produced here, and after lunch we saw them being force fed. I was glad we hadn't watched this procedure before lunch or I might not have felt like eating at all. A man holds the duck while food from a machine is pushed through a tube down the duck's throat. It takes about three seconds for each duck and, while it sounds horrible, they don't seem to mind. They crowd and push to get through the gate to the food and afterward seem to want to come back immediately for more. Every four hours day and night this goes on and after sixty days they are sent to the restaurants.

The stock farm is breeding marvelous big horses for work in the fields. Most of the horses we see on the roads and fields are small, but there are huge stallions here and most of the mares are normal size. All the animals in this commune are taken excellent care of and when I asked whether a horse that dies or gets too old to work is used for meat, they were shocked and said, no, horses live out their lives even if they can't be used, and then are buried. A man is in charge here at the stock farm.

At the flour mill another girl was head, and many of the workers were women. The village shop carried all the items anyone living the simple life of the commune could possibly need; wool, cotton, synthetics and silk, sewing and knitting materials, pots and pans, thermos jugs, china and glass, enamel basins decorated with bright flowers, in all sizes from the small size we wash our hands in to huge ones that could hold several babies or a big laundry; tools, food, both preserved and fresh. Incidently, they don't can food at home and there aren't many canning factories, but a lot is salted and pickled or dried.

Next stop was the equivalent of an old people's home, and the difference in the atmosphere compared to any I have been to in the United States is striking. Everyone was smiling and cheerful and terribly excited about our visit.

One-story buildings surround a good-sized courtyard where vegetables grow in tiny plots in the middle. Really old, decrepit men and women walked slowly about, leaning on canes, or sat on benches in the sun. We saw a room of bedridden old men, each in his own bed, watched over by a cheery young girl. We visited a blind woman in her room where she somehow manages to do everything for herself, even boil water on an oil stove. She was urged to tell us how, when she was a child, she was beaten and abused by a landlord until she lost her eyesight. Since Liberation she has been taken care of by the government. We saw the kitchen and dining room, where those who can help with serving and cleaning up. We inspected the supply rooms, one full of quilts and clothing, another of grain and flour.

Some of the old people have always lived in the vicinity, some come from other villages. A few come from farther away but have no family, so are sent here. However, no old person is forced to leave his village if he wants to stay; some arrangement is made for his care. Old, alone and poor—the frightening aspects that face so many human beings in our world. But here, though old and certainly poor, these people appeared to be enjoying security and companionship, and there were young people around, which eliminated the dreaded isolation of old age.

We visited the dispensary run by two "barefoot doctors," peasants trained as dispensary aides. They have no formal medical education, but have learned enough to be able to diagnose and treat simple ailments, the most common being colds and digestive problems. The term "barefoot" refers to the fact that they are simple people. In order to cope with the enormous problems of public health in the beginning of the revolution it was necessary to go right to the lowest level and teach people how to take care of themselves and others. These doctors can give acupuncture treatments and they showed us two cloth cases of needles in varying lengths and sizes, rather like sewing machine needles.

We saw an orchard that was mostly apple trees but had a few peach trees. The Chinese plant their trees closer together than we do and I believe they prune more heavily. Apple trees are sprayed with pesticides seven or eight times a year which doesn't seem excessive in a country where we smell DDT at every turn. They must use a great deal in the animal barns and pens because I wasn't conscious of any flies or bugs, but Harrison, who has been keeping a fly-count since his first day here, saw twelve which has brought his total up to twenty-three. When and if he gets to forty he is going to write a story about it as other reporters have said they didn't see any flies in China and he thought that was too good to be true, which is being born out. Soybeans grow between the trees on every spare bit of ground; not a usable inch is left empty.

They say there is no crime or stealing, but we noticed four strands of barbed wire around the new orchard, and on top of a brick wall surrounding a large brick building were broken pieces of glass in mortar. I didn't ask what the building was and now I'm sorry, but I hate to ask questions when I feel that people don't want to answer or might be embarrassed, and I definitely had that impression.

My main impression of this day at the commune is that there is a very strong feeling of family, of family groups. They own their own homes, have their own animals and vegetables, live a family life and have possessions, no matter if they are limited and simple. Each household pays a tiny amount for electricity (the single low-watt bulb that hangs from a wire in the middle of most of the rooms), for wood or coke for their fires, and families who live in apartments pay a small rent. There are still wells for water and holes in the ground for outdoor toilets for the houses, but apartments, as noted, have running water, flush toilets and sinks. Girls and women seem especially composed, serene and self-confident, their attitude and appearance are beautiful no matter what their features look like. Many very young women have important positions of responsibility; I sense real equality, not just lip service. Everyone has to work if he or she is able, and everyone works long and hard; no one is idle and no one gets anything for nothing, but they are secure, and certainly they look and act, not only content, but happy.

27

June 1

THIS MORNING we visited a middle school in Peking. The students are from thirteen to seventeen, come from the neighborhood and no exam is necessary to go from primary to middle school. We were very impressed at the general feeling we received from both teachers and students. While simple and drab to look at (gray is certainly the color of Peking, the old buildings, old walls, the clothes everyone wears, even the air on some days) there is a great spirit of wanting to do well, to do right, to work hard and succeed in school so that after school one can do his or her best for the country and people. "Serve the people," is the motto we hear most.

Formerly, they say, teaching used to be divorced from reality, political action and functions; "planting crops on the blackboard," for example, is one phrase used to describe an agricultural teacher who does not know one crop from another, only knows theory, not practice. In the past students could not solve practical problems, did not know anything about the fundamentals of life, of growing food, of how things they used every day were made. They despised and looked down on the peasant and factory worker, thought the intellectual was the ideal, and superior.

The main question today is, what is the point of your education, what is the point of teaching? It used to be to get good marks, get a degree; for the teacher, to acquire fame. Now it is to serve the worker and the peasants. Of course, all this talk about peasants is foreign and strange to me, as to all Americans. We don't have any peasants, never have had, and I don't feel that we differentiate between workers in factories and workers in anything else. The Chinese ask about our "workers" and I guess we can say that what we call labor is our working class, but certainly they are not repressed. The hard hats as they are sometimes called are apt to be reactionary and have very bourgeois standards. I can't help but think that people like Harrison and me are workers. He works nine to ten hours at his office five days a week and writes at home from eight to eleven or twelve o'clock at least three nights and most of every weekend. I do all the cooking for a family that ranges from two to often eight or more for supper and weekends, manage two houses, keep most of the accounts, take care of a vegetable and flower garden, do everything but the cleaning and some of the laundry, besides several other activities, so I consider myself a worker too, and an old-fashioned one—no five-day week, seven-hour day for me.

Another puzzling thing is the constant talk about "The People;" I don't know who they are, or how to differentiate who belongs to this group and who doesn't, and why. Anyway, "Liberation" is the way the Chinese refer to the Revolution, to the time when the Communists "liberated" the Chinese people from Chiang Kai-shek and the feudal system of warlords and landowners. That is why the Chinese Army

29

today is called the People's Liberation Army, the PLA. Before Liberation, students and teachers didn't have the right approach to manual labor, they looked down on it. Now students are proud to work in a factory or with the peasants in the countryside, and the teachers spend time doing all these manual things too.

The school administrators said they still feel they are in the probing and experimental stages in their schools and universities, still searching for new methods for the socialist state. Harrison asked if they could clarify the situation of schools during the Cultural Revolution. The answer was that the rebellion was against just what they had been telling us about—the leadership, the personal ambition of teachers, which was to get notice or money because of a book, and the superior attitude of the students toward peasant, worker and soldier, although they themselves were incapable of doing anything practical. This school was closed for six months during that time; soon after, the Liberation Army sent representatives to the schools and this school reopened with the same administration and students but with the idea of teaching and continuing the Revolution. The works of Mao Tsetung and Marxism and Leninism, as these ideologies are called, were the only subjects taught. Now, however, there are twelve courses, including politics, math, language, physics, chemistry, basic knowledge of agriculture, hygiene, physical culture, revolutionary art, and the whole purpose is not only to teach or learn but to serve the people.

This school used to be a British missionary school but after 1949 it became a middle school. Some of the buildings date from the British occupancy: the whole is a mixture of old and new. We visited an English language class and on the blackboard were several English words and phrases: "an announcement "; "attention please"; "Indo-China"; "Indo-Chinese peoples"; "yard"; "school yard"; "hero"; "heroic."

The class shouted in unison after the teacher, "The Indo-Chinese people are heroic people." You can't imagine the sound that comes from the classrooms. There are about fifty students in each room and they all open their mouths and yell.

In an agriculture class the teacher was lecturing about fertilizers, both chemical and organic. In the hygiene class anatomy is taught, the nature and prevention of diseases, general biological and medical knowledge, cleanliness, how to take care of their bodies. They say there are no problems of sex or morality in the school, and they add that these are social problems and taken care of by the family. It would not be appropriate to teach them here, and sex education is not necessary in this society. Affairs are frowned on, both in school and out. A clinic at the school is in charge of teaching and giving out birth control information to the teachers and adults. The necessity does not arise with students, they insist. I brought down the house when I asked if what we call "domestic arts or domestic science"—cooking, sewing—are taught in school. They laughed and said that was reserved for the family, too.

There is great emphasis on taking care of your body and being clean and healthy and quite a lot of time is spent doing exercises and calisthenics. The whole school lines up in the yard between classes and does exercises that look deceptively leisurely but are in fact positions of traditional Chinese boxing, nothing hurried or jerky but regular and controlled. Harrison thought they looked casual, but if you try to do them you realize they take learning and skill. The athletic teacher, in red sweatsuit trousers and blue top, stood on a platform in front of the students, called out directions and demonstrated his skill. He was a beautiful sight to see. The children also have a class of athletics, running and jumping over bars and gymnastics.

31

In addition to classroom teaching there are several small factories in the school. We visited one where the students were making transistors with equipment improvised and made by themselves. Since 1966 the rule has been that each student must spend a month in the factory and a month in the countryside, to learn the right approach to manual labor and to learn how to combine knowledge and practice.

Another project in which each student must join is the construction of the air raid shelter. All over this huge country underground shelters are being built. In Peking on nearly every street are huge mounds of earth that have been dug out, and piles of bricks and concrete forms for lining the tunnels. All buildings, even small houses, have shelters that connect with the main tunnels which lead away from congested areas. This is happening in every part of China, even in the countryside. They are building an underground world complete with water and necessary facilities for accommodating the entire population, 800,000,000 people—proof of how worried they are about nuclear attack, although they add it is for protection against natural disasters too. In the school yard we noticed an enormous pile of large evenly cut stones resembling huge gray bricks, and were told they are stones from the old wall that had surrounded the city. When the wall was taken down students brought the stones here, stones made by workers years ago but used to protect the rulers; now they will be used to protect the people, they said.

We noticed students with red arm bands and learned that they are Red Guards, several in each class. These Red Guards are not the same as the Red Guards who raised such havoc during the Cultural Revolution; those sprang up when students left the schools and universities and roamed through the cities and the countryside stirring things up and "making revolution," as they say. They took the law into their own hands and called themselves the Red Guards. Since the Cultural Revolution most of them have been sent to the country to live and work with the peasants. The present Red Guards are more like Boy Scouts, a purely school group. To become a Red Guard a student applies, is considered by other Guards and approved if found worthy. A Guard must work very hard, must study especially the works of Marx, Lenin and Mao, must be able to unite students. Guards take a leading role in the schools, help with disciplinary problems such as tardiness, unruliness in class, truancy. Formerly, teachers used force, now teachers and students talk to the wrong doer, or thinker, and use persuasion and education to get him or her to change. They work very hard at this method of keeping order, sometimes going to the parents in especially difficult cases.

In this school most of the parents of students are regular workers (which I suppose means factory workers), some are teachers, some doctors, a small number are from the Liberation Army, very few from former capitalist families. I have heard no mention so far, except for this vague reference, to anyone who was a rich man and not of the working class. After all, there was a lot of business and trade in China and many Chinese as well as foreign merchants, who made a great deal of money. While some left the country after Liberation, many remained. The government took over all business and banking, generally paid off the owners, who continued to work but for the government instead of themselves. I wonder what they are doing now, and what they think. Perhaps we have met some and perhaps they really are so involved with this new society that they have forgotten their past.

I can't help but be impressed with the practicality of this education though it may not be turning out many candidates for universities and Ph. D's. Because all students attending middle school must spend time in factories and the country, obviously when they finish middle school they will have gained a great deal of practical information. After graduating each girl and boy has to spend three years in the country with the peasants, in a factory with the workers, or in the army with the soldiers. Only after that can he or she go to a university for further education.

In the afternoon we visited a factory that was started around 1958 for and by housewives. They began by making the most simple and primitive kind of weight measures by hand in odd hours when they had time. In 1966 the first furnace was built by women who had gone to school to learn engineering drawing, and now they make diffusion furnaces which are necessary to the transistor industry. Of course, it is now said that there are no housewives in China, only |workers (in fact housewife is almost a dirty word). And there are not many women who stay at home to take care of their houses and families and have spare time. In the first place the homes are small, and in the second place men cook and wash as much as the women. I asked a man who has a wife and three children who did the laundry in his house and he replied, "Whoever comes home from work first." It is only the grandmothers who stay at home, but often they work in the nurseries at the factories, schools or communes. So now while most of the workers in this factory are women, they are not called housewives any more and they work on regular shifts. The output has increased yearly as new methods have been introduced and members of the Revolutionary Committee stimulate their urge to do their best and most for the country.

Later at the Peking Hotel, we watched a movie of the archeological treasures that have been unearthed in Sian, the ancient capital of the empire, dating as far back as 6000 B.C. It is hard to take in. They are so beautiful, so wonderfully preserved and so well shown in this film. There is a kneeling figure in a brocade coat holding an ingenious candle stand with a smokestack and a handle that turns to give more or less light; magnificent ceramic horses, gold objects, jeweled headdresses. Evidently a lot of these treasures were discovered by a group of Red Guards who had started digging for a public building. Harrison says he believes that the treasures of the world are buried in China; no matter where you might dig you would find something wonderful.

The next movie was about how the thoughts of Chairman Mao inspired a peasant to grow peanuts far superior to any ever previously grown in that area. This is the kind of thing we tend to laugh at and can't imagine Americans taking seriously. But in spite of the naïveté there is something touching and simple and so good about it that I can't laugh it off. And it is true, as the movie shows; this man thought a lot about how to improve his crop because he wanted to do his best and not be satisfied with the way peanuts had always been grown, so he came up with an idea of loosening the soil around each plant at a certain time to let more sun and nourishment get to the roots. It worked and everyone felt better, got more peanuts, and probably a better price.

The third movie was about the Red Flag Canal, a fantastic feat of engineering achieved almost entirely by the spirit and will of a great mass of people. Water from miles away was brought through mountains, which had to be blasted and tunneled through. Most of the work was done by hand, thousands of people swarming over the land, until finally an area that had suffered for centuries from drought and starvation and death has water to irrigate its fields and make life possible for its inhabitants. We had to leave before it was over as we were going to dine with Madame Sun Yat-sen.

Family names come first in China and women have always kept their own names when they marry, so Madame

Sun Yat-sen, as she is known to us in the West, is known in her own country simply as Soong Ching-ling. She is the widow of the founder of the Chinese Revolution and Vice Chairman of the People's Republic of China. She is also the sister of Madame Chiang Kai-shek and Madame Kung, all daughters of the American-educated Charlie Soong. There is a saying here that these three remarkable sisters were interested in the three p's: Madame Chiang, power; Madame Kung, politics; Madame Sun Yat-sen, people. Neither of us had ever met her but Harrison sends her the *Sunday Times Book Review* and *Magazine* and has corresponded with her.

A Foreign Ministry car picked us up at 6:15 at the Peking hotel where we had been watching the movies with Prof. and Mrs. John Fairbank of Harvard. After driving about twenty minutes we turned into a street along the side of a lake. We drove up to a huge closed red gate; five young army men stood outside and when the gate was opened, four more stood inside. These soldiers look so young to me, like serious children in dress-up clothes. As we went up the driveway it was just the way I imagine old-world Peking, beautiful gardens on either side and a large, handsome, traditional Chinese house at the end. A Mercedes was parked near the house and two men waited to greet us. There is a lot of handshaking here and I never know who is who or what so I put out my hand to everyone I see. A friend who lived in China before Liberation told me that she can't get over all the handshaking. In those days there was so much disease you wouldn't think of shaking hands with everyone you met; you put your hands together and made a little bow, like the Buddhist greeting. It still doesn't come naturally to her even though she agreed that we have not seen a dirty hand since we've been here, and we all know there are no more contagious diseases rampant.

We were led down a path next to the house with beautiful

roses growing beside it, into a hall, down several long corridors, past many doors, some shut, some open, and into a living room where this marvelous woman sat—short and quite round, black hair pulled straight back in a bun, gray flannel trousers, and a simple top of black silk with a white pin stripe. She has tiny hands and when she gets up you realize how small she is. In the dining room I noticed she had a cushion behind her on the chair and her feet rested on a straw stool, or mat, under the table.

When only nine years old, her father, Charlie Soong, sailed to America to live with his shopkeeper uncle in Boston, to learn the business and eventually take it over. But after several years, determined to have an education rather than continue in the family business, he went south, first to Methodist Trinity College, then to Vanderbilt University in Nashville, Tennessee. He returned to Shanghai in 1886 hoping to educate his countrymen and help his country by preaching the Methodist gospel. But before long he gave up preaching and worked for better conditions through industrialization. He imported machines and equipment, learned to install and run them, worked in factories himself. His friendship with Sun Yat-sen developed through their mutual desire to do something for China, for the masses of poor and starving. He welcomed the revolutionary ideas of his contemporary and friend, helper and supporter. He brought up his children as Christians, taught them to think for themselves, be self-reliant, and sent them to English-language schools. All three daughters went to colleges in America, E-ling and Ching-ling to Wesleyan in Macon, Georgia, Mai-ling to Wellesley. All three daughters married men who were active in the fight for nationalism in China, against the emperor and the feudal system of warlords. E-ling married Dr. Kung who became finance minister of the Nationalists; Ching-ling married her father's friend, Sun Yat-sen, the founder of the Revolution and quite a few years later, Mai-ling married Chiang Kai-shek. Working first together in the Kuomintang, the government formed to fight the emperor, Chiang broke with the Communists in 1927, two years after Sun Yat-sen's death, slaughtering them by the thousands. Madame Sun went to Russia, the other two sisters remained with their nationalist husbands. Of course at the time of the Revolution, Madame Chiang escaped to Taiwan, Madame Kung came to the United States and today only Madame Sun lives in her native China, loved and revered by her countrymen.

The guests were a Chinese couple we knew and four others we had not met before. As usual we had tea in the living room and talked for a while, then walked back through the long corridor to a huge dining room. A round table was set in the middle of the room under a bright light, with a vase of roses, which was taken away as we sat down to make space for the wonderful food. People don't eat by candle-light or dimmed light here; there is usually a lamp or chandelier over the table. There were also some heavenly peonies in the living room and this was the first time in China that I have seen flowers in a vase.

Dinner began with pigeon egg soup—clear soup with a hard but tender boiled egg in it. A bit scornfully Madame told us that President Nixon had referred to it as a quail's egg. We had Peking duck again, but this time we were spared all the supposedly delectable tidbits made out of the webbed feet and insides. The duck came complete with scallions and the paper-thin pancakes you wrap it in, the flat wheat buns you stuff it in, and a big bun on a butter plate for each person. No rice was served but there were several beautiful vegetable dishes. As each new platter was brought in, Madame rose from her chair and served Harrison, who was on her right, then the man on her left, which was the signal for the man next to me to serve me; after that everyone helped themselves. Harrison's and my places were set with knives and forks as well as chopsticks and each time I had trouble picking up a bite Madame said, "Use your fork. You won't get anything to eat if you don't." But I persisted with the chopsticks and am getting more adept at each meal. It isn't really difficult, just takes doing.

For dessert we had poor man's pudding, which is made of eight elements, but no one could remember more than four —glutinous rice, plums, red bean that looks like chocolate, and lotus pods. With this we had almond tea, which must actually be warm almond milk. As if all this were not enough, we then had the most wonderful fruit—apples and the crisp pears I have eaten only in Asia. Madame kept urging us to take the fruit home and I said I should have brought a shopping bag, that I didn't know how to carry it. She told us that in Canton in the old days when you went out to dinner, your servant came with baskets and took home for you all that you could not eat. H. told her about "doggy bags" in the United States, adding that he thought many times people ate the leftover steak for lunch the next day instead of giving it to their dogs. As we were leaving she stuffed apples and pears into my pocket book saying, "in your doggy bag," and gave me the beautiful roses that had been on the table.

She has not been feeling well because of a bad reaction to some drugs she was given last year. (She said she was sorry to say it was a woman doctor who had not tested her first to make sure the drugs were acceptable.) She has hives or shingles and is very uncomfortable, so it was especially nice of her to have us for dinner. She is a lovely, unassuming person and I feel it was one of the greatest privileges of my life to have met her.

June 2

THIS MORNING at 8:15 we drove to the Friendship Hospital here in the city to see some operations performed with only acupuncture used as anesthetic, needle anesthesia, as they call it. Increasingly in the West, we hear about acupuncture, the ancient Chinese method in which needles are inserted in the body at particular points. Since 400 B.C.—nearly twenty-five hundred years ago—this method has been used in China for treatment of all kinds of ills. About ten years ago Chinese doctors began experimenting with it as an anesthetic, and today operations are performed in every hospital in China with acupuncture used to anesthetize the strategic area. According to a government regulation, doctors must practice on themselves to find the most effective spot to insert the needles.

When we started off in the taxi our driver figured we were sick because we were going to the hospital, and drove us to the out-patient clinic. We finally got to the correct door where we were met by the director of the hospital, other doctors and personnel. The director, Dr. Chang Wei-sun, is fifty-eight years old, a pediatrician who trained in Los Angeles, the Children's Hospital and Peter Bent Brigham Hospital in Boston, and interned at Bellevue in New York City. He is a terribly nice, friendly, simple man. We followed him up a flight of stairs and into a big room where there were chairs and sofas for the visitors and hospital staff. There was quite a crowd: two "overseas Chinese" dentists from Hawaii (that is how the Chinese-born who lives outside of China proper are referred to); several handsome ladies from the British embassy, including Mrs. Anthony Royal, whose husband is over here to see about trade between Britain and China; a Japanese girl married to an Englishman; a young blonde girl who had done some work for Cy Sulzberger in Hong Kong last year before she came here with her husband; three cameramen who were to film the operations for a British documentary; a middle-European woman doctor; and quite a few other men and women whom I never did identify.

We had tea while Dr. Chang told us about the hospital and the operations we were about to see. The hospital has six hundred beds, is a general hospital for that district of the city. It provides care for the people in the district; well over two thousand are seen in the out-patient clinic and patients are referred from the country when they cannot get the necessary treatment and care. People pay for their treatment, but if they can't, their commune or factory pays; medical and hospital care is never denied anyone. Doctors receive salaries about once again as much as ordinary workers' salaries. Their training is free, as is all education.

Dr. Chang told us about their treatment of cancer, about the same as everywhere; operations, radium, drugs and chemical therapy, except that they use acupuncture to re-

41

lieve pain. Their attitude seems more realistic than ours and it sounds as if doctors are with their patients a great deal more than they are in our hospitals. For abortions, which can be had by any woman on request, but which they say are performed almost entirely on married women, the suction method is used more than any other. For childbirth no drugs are given as they are in our hospitals because it is a "natural" function, but if the labor is prolonged and difficult, acupuncture can be used to ease the discomfort.

Someone asked about psychiatry, whether there were psychiatrists and how do they cope with mental illness. The answer is there are no psychiatrists. While the Chinese recognize insanity as such, they feel that there isn't much time or place for neurosis in their society. Most people are too busy to be neurotic, and if they do have mental or emotional problems, working hard and concentrating on the thoughts of Mao Tse-tung usually eliminates them. This conversation reminded me of the men I met in the Chinese embassy in Ottawa. They had asked me about psychiatry in America and I was trying to explain that sometimes people do become upset and confused and it can be a great help to talk to an impartial person, especially one who has studied human behavior. They just couldn't take it in, and one of them said, "A doctor who cures by talking—I don't understand that at all."

The operations scheduled for today were removal of an ovarian cyst, thyroid cyst, hernia repair and cataract. Men and women repaired to separate rooms where we changed into sterile hospital suits, hats, sandals and surgical masks. One of the English ladies asked me which operation I preferred to watch and I said I thought I would look for my husband and stay with him, watch what he watched. She replied, in that marvelous British accent, "Oh, you'll never find him in that get-up." We had another cup of tea in our changing room and the four patients walked in to be introduced. They all said they had had long talks with their doctors, they understood just what was going to happen during the operations and they were not afraid; they felt everyone was interested in helping them and they were hoping to be able to help the doctor to help them. That isn't as strange as it sounds because if a patient is conscious he can help a lot by coughing, for instance, to let the doctor see what pushes where and how much, and whether stitches will hold.

There were two operating rooms on either side of the hall and we walked freely between them. The patients were put on the operating tables and the acupuncture needles applied, seven in the eyebrows and forehead for the ovarian cyst operation.

In some hospitals now the needles are attached to electric wires to keep them twirling instead of being twirled by hand. Evidently it doesn't hurt at all when they are inserted; if done skillfully you feel nothing, not even the jab that sometimes hurts when a doctor takes blood out of your finger or your ear, or the prick of the needle when you have a shot. I know a woman who had acupuncture treatment in Paris for arthritis pains. She had twelve needles inserted in her thigh and as she was nervous about it, did not look. She was waiting for something to happen and said to her husband, "When is the doctor going to put in the needles?" And he replied, "They are all in." She had never felt a thing, not even a sensation.

They waited about twenty minutes before commencing the operations. A beautiful woman doctor performed the ovarian cyst operation assisted by two other women, one a full-fledged doctor and one a student. The student handed instruments to the doctors, and several nurses helped her. The other operations were done by men doctors, each with a student assistant. This is part of applying Chairman Mao's dictum of practice along with theory: medical students are put right in the operating rooms, always with an experienced surgeon, so they can learn from him and "reality" in the beginning as well as through classroom sudy. The medical course has been cut to three years, which they feel is adequate under these circumstances.

I found Harrison in spite of his disguise, but even beside him I was afraid I would disgrace myself and my country by fainting because it was so hot; and while I am a Red Cross nurses' aide I have never actually watched an operation. But there was no smell of ether or any of the nauseating and faint-making smells of our hospitals, and I managed all right. I didn't stand close and gaze into the body cavities, so avoided seeing too much blood and gore. And I did feel that if I watched operations every day for a week I'd get used to it. While I could never be casual about watching a human body cut open and blood gush out, it wouldn't be so startling. The patients were conscious. The only one I couldn't be sure about by looking at him was the man having a cataract removed, as his face was all covered up and only the one eye showed through the opening in the cloth; but I heard the doctor talking to him and caught some mumblings back. As in all operations, nurses sat by the patients, keeping watch over blood pressure and pulse, and, of course, the needles; and, because the patients were conscious, asking them how they felt and occasionally pouring driblets of tea from tiny pots into their mouths. There was no fear, no smell, it all seemed very natural. The girl with the ovarian cyst said that when the doctor made the incision in her abdomen it felt as if a feather had brushed over her stomach. In abdominal and deep inside operations there is a sensation, though no pain, as if your insides were being pulled and handled, which naturally they are, and it can be unpleasant. But this patient talked during her operation, and

44

said she felt "lighter" when a cyst the size of a grapefruit was cut out. It was passed around in a basin for all to see, as was the cataract and thyroid cyst.

We said goodbye to the patients as they were wheeled to the elevators to go back to the wards where they would receive the same post-operative care as in our hospitals, except they get more attention because they have more nurses and help than we have. The cataract patient would stay two weeks or longer, and I believe such cases go home much sooner with us. The hospital was shabby but clean. The atmosphere was simple and natural and seemed related to human beings, with none of the big impersonal factory quality of so many of our hospitals.

Over and over we are impressed with the spirit here: from doctors and nurses to the men and women who sweep the corridors and clean up the operating room; from members of the government to taxi drivers; from the teachers we have met to the men who work in our hotel. There is a dignity in every human being, a sense of his own worth and a place in the scheme of things, and the most extraordinary feeling of care, connection with, and concern for one's fellowman.

June 3

EVERY TIME we go on one of these long trips I miss a birthday I hate to miss. My mother-in-law once said, "It is never
the right time to have a baby or take a trip," and the latter
has certainly been true for me. On Curtis's fifteenth birthday a few years ago we were in Mongolia; today Rosina is
twenty-nine. She was born during World War II—I remember so well, there wasn't a father around to visit the
new babies and mothers in the hospital, they were all off in
the army or navy.

This morning we visited Tsinghua University, a scientific
and technological university that can be compared to the
Massachusetts Institute of Technology, on the outskirts of
Peking. Our tour began with the usual greeting at the door,
tea in a large room with a group of teachers and several
students. As we have come to expect, we were introduced to
the members of the Revolutionary Committee, who are the
administration nowadays. When the Red Guard movement

overthrew the existing administrations in towns, schools, factories, and other institutions, so-called Revolutionary Committees were set up to take their place. Usually the committee included a few Red Guards, a few PLA men, and a sprinkling of the former administration which had taken the side of the Cultural Revolution. Later on, after the top personnel of most institutions had gone to the May 7 schools where, as they say, they came to recognize the errors of their former thoughts and ways, they returned to their old posts and often joined the Revolutionary Committee. Here at Tsinghua, they are trying to get the university going again and raise the enrollment to where it was before the Cultural Revolution. This will take several more years.

We visited some of the factory rooms and some classrooms, then returned to the big room, this time with about ten or twelve students, for discussion. Among them was a boy from the navy, another from the army and a girl who is in charge of a boiler in one of the university factories. They were all nice looking, extremely healthy, spoke without embarrassment, and with great assurance and conviction. They began by saying they were against the Vietnam war and we said we were too, that many Americans were and always had been from the beginning. They said they supported the student movement and asked about students and workers' strikes in the United States. They understand the antiwar demonstrations and the rebelling against faculty, administration and trustees, against the established way, but no one in a socialist or communist society can fathom that our labor, especially the leaders, is reactionary, capitalistic, in favor of the Vietnam war, racist and antiblack. H. asked them if they knew about our drug problem and they answered that they had not heard of it until the doctor who accompanied Nixon to China had asked about drugs in the hospital these students attend and had spoken of drugs in the United States. This was the first they had heard of the problem and they are genuinely appalled; they can't understand why anyone, especially young people, would want to take drugs—"it's so very bad for one's health." There is a great emphasis on health and cleanliness in Mao's teachings, and it is obvious everywhere that it has made a big impression. One girl said she had never seen an opium pipe except in an exhibition hall, and I believe it is true that there are no drugs or users, let alone addicts, in China today.

To have accomplished this is a miracle, especially in a country where for years a large percentage of the population took drugs regularly. I wonder why we, in the United States, can't follow their example. The steps they took are obvious; they stopped growing poppies, stopped the manufacture of drugs, and arrested the sellers. I have heard Americans say that when the Communists took over, users and addicts were arrested and put in jail, but this is not true. The government took the attitude that this was everybody's problem, that everybody should help the victims to overcome their disease, and they were worked on by their families and friends, by public opinion. They were put in hospitals, talked to and persuaded to stop. And now there are none. It sounds so simple, and yet I believe we could do the same. The first step would be to take the profit out of the drug business; the second would be education—to teach people of all ages the dangers of drugs. Then if somehow the American people could be persuaded to feel more responsible for each other, to realize that what happens to anyone of us affects our whole society, to feel that all men really are brothers, that, as the Chinese often say to us, "We are one big family"— then, the rest should follow naturally.

They had also heard of rock and roll but had never actually listened to any and didn't want to; they preferred to live their type of Spartan life, up at 5:30, working hard all day and listening to their own revolutionary music. They said that their music reflects their life, their heroes and athletes. Learning revolutionary operas and music is a way to learn from these heroes, and it helps them to work for the Revolution and for all the people in the world. Harrison asked them how they could be so sure they would not like it if they have never heard it. They answered that while they have not heard American music, they have heard what they think is the Russian equivalent of rock and roll and they think it is ridiculous, not related to reality, and that there is no place in their life for such bourgeois music. Such music has a lot to do with drugs and makes people degenerate, one said, rather than wanting to work for the Revolution and serve the proletariat.

One girl said that before the Cultural Revolution the arts were dominated by the revisionists, and were not in conformity with the new life in China. Now music, art and literature must serve the worker, the peasant and the soldier, must depict the life of these people. The name itself, rock and roll, indicates it would not serve them. This girl said that after seeing "On the Docks," a revolutionary opera, she was so inspired she was able to work much better, and I think she is right that rock and roll doesn't inspire hard work and dedication to the working people. H. suggested that President Nixon might have felt in reverse the way they do about our music, that he might have not wanted to see the revolutionary ballet, "The Red Detachment of Women," but that he had been a good sport and given it a try. They answered that while he may not have appreciated the political aspects of the story, they thought he probably enjoyed the music.

H. suggested that their attitude is chauvinistic and they answered, "This is our view." They believe that singing the "Internationale" shows they are not chauvinistic. They do hear contemporary foreign music, from Albania, North Vietnam, North Korea, and Cambodia, now that Sihanouk, the ousted ruler, is in Peking. These are the only foreign countries they are at all familiar with and when asked if they would like to go abroad they answered they would like to visit these, their sister socialist countries, and the United States.

For recreation after class they have dancing, art, music—they even compose their own music. All their dances are folk dances, nobody wants to dance with just one person. H. asked them if they had ever danced with just one other boy or girl and they said no, and they couldn't imagine it. He asked them what they would do if they came to America and went to a dance and everyone else was dancing together. They answered they were sure their American hosts would be polite enough to understand them and not insist they do something they didn't want to do. They have an amazing coolness and assurance, no self-doubt here.

In the schools and universities there are classes in Chinese, which must mean language study. In order to read easily it is necessary to know three or four thousand characters, so it must take even the Chinese years to learn properly; one character can have many meanings depending solely on the pronunciation. I would think that after learning Chinese anything would be a snap, but our interpreter told us that a friend of his had trouble learning English, that some of our sounds were very confusing to him. When he said goodbye to someone going off on a trip and thought he was saying "Bon Voyage," he would say enthusiastically, "bottle of wine, bottle of wine." To write properly must take years of practice too. I watch Yao Wei taking notes at our interviews, and it is incredible how fast he makes the signs that seem so unfathomable to me—as quickly as we write our simple letters. Everything is written down and not just by him; always two or three others, plus H. and me, are busy writing also. English study now is limited to language, and no longer includes literature. Primarily they need people who can speak well to be interpreters, and they practice with phrases such as we heard being shouted in the middle school: "The Indo-Chinese people are heroic people"; "Down with Imperialists, Revisionists, Capitalists"; and "Long Live the Chinese Communist Party." We see such slogans on the blackboards. So far, I have seen no sign of any literature other than Mao's writings, Mao philosophy, and no history other than Chinese. In the kindergartens the children begin early with *The Little Red Soldier,* a tiny picture book, and in the drawing classes that I have seen, everyone copies the picture the teacher draws on the board, as exactly as possible. There are lots of what they call classes in factory, in which they make parts for transistors and other mechanical components with more or less homemade factory equipment.

At dinner with some Chinese friends we discussed the art and music of today's China. It is apparently true that, according to Mao's famous speech at Yenan in 1942, there is nothing written, composed, or produced that is not relevant to the worker, the peasant and the soldier—the artist serves the people. And there is no underground for circulating works of art and literature that are not approved by the government, the way there is in Russia. In fact, I wonder where the artists and writers are; we have still to meet one.

June 4

THIS MORNING was leisurely. I even went down to the dining room and had some eggs. Usually I have just fruit and
coffee in our room while H. goes down. It gives me a little
time alone to get ready for the day, which usually starts at
8:00 or 8:15.

The light and airy dining room has different size tables,
some round, some long and narrow, some small and square
like a card table, so any number of guests, or parties, can be
accommodated. All tables are covered with plain white
cloths; a few are set in western fashion with knives and
forks; most have chopsticks, saucers, and bowls. Paper napkins cut in half, or even quartered, stand in a glass like flowers in a vase, next to containers of sugar, salt, pepper, soy
sauce (which doesn't taste anything like American soy
sauce). Sometimes wet napkins are given us after meals in
this hotel, sometimes not, but it is the general custom to use
them at the beginning and end, and often during, every

meal. Waiters pass them on a tray and hand them out with tongs.

Menus are western or Chinese and are written in both languages. None of the waiters or waitresses speak English but one waiter says "Good morning" at all times of day, asks "Western or Chinese?" at each meal, pronounces and understands some English names of food, soup, eggs, pineapple, strawberries (which are fresh now and simply divine). We use chopsticks except at breakfast. Harrison is an old hand with them and I do passably if people don't stare at me. But when I feel those amused, though worried, eyes, I can't get food from the big plate to my saucer, and from there to my mouth, without dropping each piece several times. Waiters come forward with forks but I refuse to give up. If I'm not nervous I can pick up peanuts, peas and even slippery mushrooms successfully. Like most things in life, it takes practice and confidence.

In the hotel lobby a little shop sells food, souvenirs and things a traveler might need such as toothpaste, soap (though this hotel supplies very nice soap), cold cream in tiny tin boxes, and excellent detergent in plastic bags. Souvenirs include gloves, scarves and fans; carved bone and ivory bracelets and ornaments; tiny paper lanterns that we will hang on our Christmas tree; sweaters, handkerchiefs. Food consists of fresh fruit every day, apples, oranges, cherries, pears and once in a while pineapple; chocolate and tea.

Everyone who works here is terribly friendly. One of the men on our floor says, very fast, "How are *you*?" every time we get out of the elevator or see him in the hall. And everybody smiles and nods even if they don't have such a big vocabulary in our language. This is a pleasant hotel and we are comfortable and happy here.

We went to the Forbidden City (The Imperial City) with our guide and Dick and Helen Dudman, who have just arrived in this hotel. He is the journalist of the St. Louis *Post Dispatch* who was captured by the Vietcong in Cambodia last year and held prisoner for forty days. He was released along with several others, but I believe there are twenty or thirty missing correspondents who have never been heard of since they disappeared.

It is hard to describe the Chinese palaces. I have seen many grand and gorgeous sights on our travels—the palace buildings in Cambodia, the Taj Mahal, Temples in Sikkim and Japan and what are left in Mongolia, but I have never even imagined the splendor and extent of the Chinese buildings. Built of wood, decorated and painted in brilliant colors, with carved marble and stone steps and terraces, furnished with magnificent thrones and tables, benches, stools, cupboards, mirrors, art objects, they are far more elaborate and rich than anything I have ever seen; they must be the most fabulous in the world. The Imperial Palaces, containing more than nine thousand rooms, are inside the big red wall and cover about two hundred acres. You go through a gate in the huge wall and through another gate which leads to the Hall of Supreme Harmony, the largest of all the palace buildings. As you go out the back of each palace another symmetrical arrangement of buildings greets you, all in perfect proportion. And though they are not all named some kind of harmony, there is harmony between and among them, each one leading to another, bigger or smaller, maybe slightly different in layout and size, but always in perfect sympathy with the whole.

From the Hall of Supreme Harmony you go to the Hall of Middle Harmony and the Hall of Preserving Harmony; then to the Palace of Heavenly Purity, the Hall of Union, the Palace of Earthly Tranquility, the Hall of Royal Peace, the Hall of Mental Cultivation, the Hall of the Absolute, formerly called the Palace of Endlessness and later the Palace of

Blessings, the Hall of Manifest Origin, the Palace of Eternal Spring, the Palace of Blessings to Mother Earth, originally named Myriad Peace Palace; the Palace of Gathering Excellence and the Hall of Manifest Harmony, which is the Gate of Gathering Excellence rebuilt. The emperors were often carried in enormous elaborate sedan chairs from one palace and hall to another: one where they talked to their ministers, one where they handed out decrees, another where they examined the seed for the next harvest, others where they did the governmental work, and still others where they lived and relaxed with their families.

In the official pamphlet the description includes, "the grandeur and magnificence of the structure fully demonstrate the wisdom, talent and highly accomplished building technique of China's ancient laboring people." I feel the emperors who ordered it built deserve some praise, too, for their taste, love of beauty and impeccable sense of proportion and design, qualities that are not much in evidence in the new buildings we have seen so far.

In the Imperial Gardens of ancient cedars and strange rock formations rather than flowers, hundreds of people were eating picnic lunches they had brought with them. All seemed to be family groups, all generations from babies to grandmothers. I didn't see one piece of trash anywhere.

Some of the palaces are now museums and contain a magnificent collection of ancient works of art that have been discovered in the recently opened tombs, many that were in the film we saw the other afternoon. It was like meeting old friends to see them "in the flesh." Among the treasures are the famous jade suits, made of dark green squares linked together to make suits like armor to completely cover the dead bodies of the emperor and empress. This is the kind of royal gesture that is so unbelievable to me; I can't imagine putting all that jade in a tomb. Room after room held further treasures, dishes and bowls and the well-known ceramic horses; many gold utensils, including a large urn that was made for one of the emperors to keep the hair left in his mother's hairbrush after she—or a slave perhaps—had brushed her hair. (He must have had the Oedipus complex of all time.) Here are pictures made of feathers so skillfully dyed and applied in designs that they look as if they were paintings, and headdresses so elaborate and bejeweled it is hard to see how anyone could hold her or his head up. Through room after room we walked, goggle-eyed at the luxury and richness. I wonder what the average Chinese thinks, a man or woman who has probably no more than two sets of clothes, exactly alike and exactly like what everyone else wears, no jewelry except maybe a practical sensible wristwatch, not even a wedding ring, and whose worldly possessions include only the bare necessities for life. One item which amazed me—for I had never seen or heard of such a thing—was a mat woven of ivory strips. It is flexible and was used by emperors and empresses to sleep on, the way Chinese sleep on straw mats when it is boiling hot.

After lunch, again with the Dudmans, we drove out to the Summer Palace, a huge area with several lakes, the famous bridge of seventeen arches, islands, palaces, pagodas, all rising up from the lake and going in stages up to the top of Longevity Hill. The emperor who kept his mother's hair strands redid a lot of the Summer Palace grounds and gave the hill its name in honor of her sixtieth birthday. It seemed more like a mountain as we climbed the thousands of steps of marble and crawled through the tunnels hacked out of the natural rock. Here I saw the first signs of refuse, papers and cigarette butts, human feces, and a strong smell of urine. This makes me wonder whether the Chinese are neat and tidy naturally or whether, if and when, in the future they have as much paper and tin for every day consumption as we have, they will litter their country in the same way. It seems as if cleanliness has been drummed into them for keeps when you consider that even in the cities, many households have only a pump in the public courtyard for water. Obviously they have to wash in basins with water they have carried, then heated. But up to now I have not seen a dirty person or anyone I would feel uncomfortable to shake hands with or sit next to. The only B.O. I have smelled here was on an American.

Though the gardens were open to the public in 1924, there has been a lot of restoration since, and the whole park is popular all year round with swimming, boating and skating in season. There was a nice holiday atmosphere, which is comforting to see because no one in China has a real two- or three-week vacation the way we have. They have several two-day holidays throughout the year, Chinese New Year for instance, all in all about eight days. Many people were in rowboats, a few swimming, and many in the bigger excursion boats. And hundreds, or maybe thousands, were just enjoying the old emperor's summer place, strolling on the two-mile covered walk, climbing up to the topmost pagoda, or just sitting with children and grandchildren.

I am surprised to see so many women whose feet were bound when they were children, women who don't look terribly old; I had imagined all were dead by now. Of all the dreadful things people have done to each other in the course of human history, binding a little girl's feet seems one of the most horrible. The toes were turned under when the child was small, three to six; generally they had to be soaked to make them soft and pliable, but sometimes the bones had to be broken to make this possible. Then they were bound tightly, the bandage being tightened gradually. The object was to have the smallest possible foot (three inches was considered ideal) and some women never could really walk at all, had to be helped or carried everywhere. The deformity gave a twisting to the gait that was considered sexy and alluring, and if a woman was immobilized it was all right because what would she do anyway? The paradox to me is that the country people did this also, and how could a woman work the way peasant women had to work in this condition? To see women now, about my age, with these tiny little shoes, walking as if it still hurt and having to use a cane, is a terrible sight. But I see them everywhere, wheeling grandchildren, carrying heavy loads and parcels; and we met one old lady, being helped, really pulled, by two younger members of her family, struggling on her doll-like feet up the last few steps to the very top of the highest pagoda.

Tonight when we came back from supper we found straw mats on our beds which, though not ivory like the emperor's, are cool and fresh. I can't help but wonder how they are cleaned, especially in a hotel where people come and go.

June 5

IN THE MORNING we visited a generator factory that employs about five thousand workers, one thousand of them women, just outside the city. This factory is like a commune in that it has its own nurseries for working mothers' babies, kindergartens, primary and middle schools, a clinic, hospital and shop. At least thirty babies were in the nursery, all dressed in bright colors and excessively bundled up considering the weather, which I find exhaustingly hot. Some were asleep on a big community *kang*, some were being fed with a bottle, others were in cribs. It must be comforting for a mother to know her baby is in this big airy room with doting grandmotherly women to take care of him while she works.

At a nursery for three-year-olds about twenty children sat in tiny chairs clapping as we walked in. We receive this greeting wherever we go, in schoolrooms, factories and communes. They say that with a language barrier it is easier to clap your hands on meeting than utter words no one understands or to stand awkwardly doing nothing. It is a little like a Buddhist greeting. In another room each child had a crib with a blanket neatly folded at the bottom, a tiny basin and a washrag hanging from a hook above it, all so tidy and minute it made me think of Beatrix Potter's Mrs. Tittlemouse.

While these children go home at night, many Chinese parents leave very young children in nurseries and kindergartens to board through the week and have them at home only on their day off. I believe this routine is primarily followed by government workers and people in the cities, not generally in communes and villages. A man told me his child of four or five comes home only one day a week and that she really prefers to be at her boarding kindergarten, she can't wait to get back after her visits home. I said I should think his wife would hate it and he replied that as she worked all day and sometimes at night, it is really a much better arrangement all around. Obviously it destroys, or eliminates, any intimacy between parents and children and gives the children at their most impressionable age to the state.

The children in the kindergarten performed various dances that are put on professionally and these four- and five-year-olds were pretty professional, too. With faces painted bright red and eyes rimmed with heavy black, they looked as if they had gotten into their mothers' cosmetics (something that couldn't happen here). One dance was about a Tibetan soldier and the girls who took away his laundry and did it to help him; another portrayed two Mongolian girls taking care of sheep. The costumes were bright and gay, authentic Tibetan and Mongolian. Master of ceremonies was a boy of four, self-assured and managerial. He marched toward us before each act, announced it in a loud piercing voice, marched back to his seat and watched each child carefully to be sure everything went according to directions. Here we saw examples of how even the smallest children are protective and solicitous of each other, as well as making sure everyone is doing the right thing; you can feel helpfulness and care even in these tiny tots.

Living quarters are provided for most of the workers in this factory: the housing is not completed yet and some workers bicycle back and forth from the city every day. The flats are big and airy, not very aesthetically pleasing to my eye but certainly adequate and clean. Most families have two or three rooms; generally children seem to sleep separately. The beds are regular-sized and each flat has a bathroom with running water, flush toilet and tub, all made of heavy dark material that looks like stone. The kitchens have sinks made of the same substance, and stoves of bricks in which coal briquettes are burned. Nothing is attractive; everything is stark and spotless.

The people we met looked and acted happy, busy, pleased with life, and proud to be part of the community and of China today. Everyone works, the family ties are still strong, the older couples have on the average four children, the younger ones have two and think that is enough.

We lunched with Ambassador and Mrs. Valdez, their daughter and another couple from the Peruvian embassy. I especially wanted Harrison to meet them as they had been so nice to me on the trip from Hong Kong to Peking. The ambassador has been troubled with insomnia and he has had two treatments of acupuncture—he went for the third right after our lunch. He told us that the first treatment lasted only five minutes and that night he slept like a baby. The next treatment took twenty minutes and I believe the one today was for twenty minutes, too. It will be interesting to know if the good effects continue.

June 6

THIS MORNING at ten we called on Prince Sihanouk, the ex-
iled ruler of Cambodia. Harrison has always wanted to meet
him. In 1966 when we were in Cambodia, Sihanouk was in
France taking his yearly cure, and after H's trip to Hanoi in
1967, they didn't meet either. We drove to a big red gate in
a big gray wall, guarded by three PLA soldiers. We had to
get out; our taxi was not permitted to enter what used to be
the old French embassy compound. The soldiers motioned
us through and we walked in attractive grounds with several
buildings, pretty planting, a big fountain, and birds singing
sweetly, a sound I haven't heard here before. We didn't
know where to go and there was no one to greet us, so we
headed for what seemed the main building and went in the
huge glass side door. Three enormous yellow vases stood in
the foyer, but no sign of life. A trim young man emerged
from a room on the left and scurried by us, in his shirt-
sleeves. In a few moments he came out of another door, ele-

gant in a dark suit, trim and chic compared to the baggy looks of the Chinese, and led us up a large, elaborately carved dark wood staircase. At the top stood His Highness, bowing and smiling. He also looked elegant and chic and he ushered us into a bright room with a sofa and a half circle of chairs. A vase on the table in front of the sofa held an exquisite arrangement of flowers, a large white peony surrounded by varicolored roses, pink, white, yellow, red, and three articles made out of silver in the typical Cambodian style—a round cigarette box, ash tray, and a lighter with carved relief of a Cambodian dancing girl, (an Aspara). A Chinese man with a Mao button brought us little glasses of grapefruit juice (I don't think they have grapefruit here so it must have been canned) and tea, which he replenished several times during our visit. A plate of dainty biscuits was on the table and His Highness rose many times to offer them to us.

He talked for two hours about his country, about how he had tried so hard to keep it neutral, which we were well aware of in 1966; about the government that threw him out and how corrupt it is, about how President Nixon had said the United States was invading Cambodia to clean out the Communist hideaways that even he, Nixon, admitted were not very extensive; and how the Communists now control far more territory than they did at that time. Sihanouk said, "We don't worry about supplies. We can buy all the American supplies we need from the corrupt Lon Nol army," and told us how the Lon Nol army sells the supplies the United States gives it to the Communist troops, (who, though they used to oppose him, are now loyal to Sihanouk) for American dollars that are given to them by the Chinese just for this purpose. The Chinese get the dollars in their limited foreign trade as all international trade is carried on in dollars or British pounds. The Cambodians loyal to Sihanouk even buy United States uniforms, and the supplies, which include medicine, food, raw materials for ammunition and guns are often delivered by the Lon Nol soldiers to the Communists in United States Army trucks.

This is what is so tragic all through Southeast Asia where we are involved. We hand out enormous sums of money and goods of every kind of the regimes that our government arbitrarily decides it wants to support, and the money is not always used for what we intend. It was the same with Chiang Kai-shek and every one admits that now; he used American aid for his own army to fight the Chinese Communists, not the Japanese. And the corrupt governments in Saigon and Phnom Penh are using our aid to make money for themselves and are selling the supplies we give them to the people we are fighting against. It doesn't make much sense. Sihanouk also told us that he had asked to see President Nixon when he was in Peking, and Nixon refused to see him. This I find shocking and uncivilized.

We had a delightful visit and felt sad and nostalgic when we left. He gave us some of his records, two modern red and black Chinese vases, and a stack of literature about Cambodia and the war. He has written a new song that is being recorded here but unfortunately the record won't be ready before we leave. His songs are romantic and he says it is hard to get a Chinese who can sing them appropriately because their music at the moment is militaristic and nonromantic, which is putting it mildly.

There are some aspects of this visit to China that remind me of the other communistic countries I have been to, the Soviet Union and Mongolia. For example, we can't really do anything without a guide; even if we knew the language, we wouldn't be able to get off on our own and talk to anyone frankly. Every day we have a program and we go where we're taken and talk to the people who it is planned for us to talk to. There are always Red Guards with the school children, and members of the Revolutionary Committee or PLA with everyone else, so even if a Chinese wanted to say something a bit out of line, he couldn't. However, so far I haven't seen anyone who seemed to be doing anything but following, living and breathing the party line with the most fervent enthusiasm and spirit.

We hear much less about "our beloved Chairman Mao" than I had expected. We see slogans here and there on buildings and posts, (at the telegraph office where H. goes to send messages to the paper a sign in big red characters reads, "The force that is leading us forward is the Chinese Communist Party"), but there aren't half as many as there used to be. There are very few statues of the Chairman such as the one in the airport, a huge white statue that makes me think of some of the pop art I have seen in the United States, strange plaster-of-Paris life-size figures, which seem equally inartistic. Also about the only people who wear Mao buttons are the workers in the hotel; others, many among the higher officials, wear "Serve the People" buttons. And so far I have seen only one person with a little red book— one of the observers of the operations in the Friendship Hospital.

June 7

CHINA HAS STARTED diplomatic relations with Greece. Of all the reactionary governments, this seems to me one of the worst and I am surprised and depressed. Somehow I had expected the Chinese to be more moral than other countries in their world dealings, and it is disillusioning to realize that they are not.

In the morning we drove out to a "May 7th School," east of Peking. These schools are more like camps and so named because on May 7, 1966, Chairman Mao ordered them set up as places where everyone, especially intellectuals and those who knew nothing of agriculture, factory production and military affairs, could learn of these things. On October 4, 1968, he reiterated these instructions saying that the broad mass of "cadres" (they use this word constantly to identify a party worker) must rotate regularly to the countryside, must participate in manual labor to gain this experience, excusing only the weak, the sick and the old. I have had the idea that these schools are prisons or detainment camps where people who didn't toe the line were sent to be reeducated. I guess that goes on in some, but in the school we visited it seems it is a privilege to be accepted; in theory, everyone *wants* to come for the required six months to learn about the wonders of hog breeding and manual labor.

On arriving we sat around a big table and drank tea while members of the administration, accompanied by several students and workers, told us about this school. Each ministry has its own May 7th school; this one, formed in 1968, is attached to the East Peking government. The directors of the school were appointed by the Central Cultural Revolutionary Committee and they (the directors) together with elected members from the school body, make up the Revolutionary Committee. There are fifty administrative and technical personnel, and some full-time workers in the factory where they make water buckets. Members of the Revolutionary Committee from the school body change frequently as people return to their former posts, but how long directors stay is decided by the District Party Committee.

In 1968 there were only barren fields where this school is situated. One thousand students lived in tents or in the nearby villages and they built everything with their own hands; many one-story buildings, where they eat, sleep, study; nice brick buildings with tile roofs. I asked how they could build houses without knowing anything about carpentry or putting on a roof, and of course, they couldn't. There were then, as now, regular workers whose main purpose, they say, is to teach the students how to do these things and to train them to be proletarian workers so that they will be able to overcome bureaucracy and revisionism. In four years the inmates of this school have opened up several hundred acres of erstwhile arid land, all without the aid of farm machinery, and now grow many vegetables in addi-

67

tion to raising hogs, which is still the main project.

There are 500 students, 400 on a half-year basis. Students apply to a May 7th School and have to be approved by their superiors; this school has never had any but spontaneous applications and cannot take all who apply. (I didn't understand this because if everyone has to go to one of these places every year how can an application be spontaneous? Maybe this particular school is first choice for many people because of its location near Peking and not miles off in the middle of nowhere. I couldn't get an answer that satisfied me about this.) Most of the students here are teachers, a few are office and factory workers. Most are here for six months though we understand that some people go to May 7th schools for just one month, particularly government people who, I imagine, can't be spared from their regular work for very long. Most of them have no knowledge of building or agriculture when they come here, 70 percent have had no experience in manual labor. Many have worked or taught in positions of authority where they issued orders; here teachers are taught, they learn from the peasant and take orders from him; here they feel their own knowledge has been limited and where formerly they have looked down on the peasant, now they see how much he knows that they don't. Their whole point of view, their whole world outlook, changes, they told us.

The schedule is in three parts: 1) the study of Marx, Engels, Lenin and Mao's thoughts; 2) manual work; 3) participation in production units in the vicinity, which means going out to work with the peasants. No matter how much manual labor they do, if they stay only in the school they will have no relationship with the peasants.

Some time each day is spent studying; at the moment the teacher-students are reading Engels, which none of them had ever studied before. They are learning how to promote revolution, have come to see why the line of Liu Shao-ch'i was wrong. How true is Mao's thought—a phrase repeated often—the heroes are the masses, "The People," not individuals. Here at this school the students learn to understand "the people," to know their motives so they will be better able to serve them. One must not separate oneself from the masses, must not be divorced from the peasant, worker and soldier, it leads to bureaucracy. Here everyone is equal, everyone—students, teachers, administrators, workers—goes to regular meetings, everyone puts forward criticisms and suggestions. Besides studying and going out to work with the peasants, they grow all their own vegetables, raise hogs and chickens and feed themselves entirely.

All students make some progress although, of course, it differs with each person. No certificates of attendance or merit are given out but each student makes his own summary and evaluation of his work, which is exchanged and discussed with other students and with the teachers. Problems of discipline do not arise as all the students are adults. Husbands and wives do not come to May 7th schools together but students can go home (if they can get there) on the two days every two weeks set aside for rest. While at school students receive their regular pay from the regular jobs to which they return after the six months, but they can be transferred to other jobs for various reasons if the Party Committee of the East District so decides, or if they are needed because of a vacancy or some emergency demand.

After this long description of life in this school, we were told that nothing is perfected yet, changes in the content of study continue to be examined and that the ideal of these schools is for the student to benefit morally, politically, intellectually; to really become self-sufficient.

We walked to the fields and met a group of girls and a

few young men tending tomato plants, pruning and weeding
accurately. A few weeks ago these people knew nothing
about growing vegetables. At the hog pens we saw many
healthy pigs of all ages, cleaned and cared for by happy-
looking men and women who normally are teachers and
white collar workers. Before lunch I made a trip to the
women's toilet, a Chinese version of an outhouse. You don't
sit on a typical Asian toilet, you squat over an oblong-shaped
bowl, which has water for flushing the same as western toilets. Generally it is set in a platform raised a step or two
from the floor. Better ones are made of white porcelain and
have a splash-guard, I guess you'd call it, at one end. Some
in the commune apartments are made of dark cement or
stone. Some that are indoors, I am told, do not have water to
flush but the contents are siphoned out into the night soil
trucks and carts, taken to special dumps to ferment, then
used as fertilizer. Generally, in modern hotels, the toilets are
western, sometimes in the public ladies rooms there are both
styles.

This outdoor toilet was enclosed by a brick and mud wall,
had two rows, at right angles, of oblong holes in the ground,
about ten in all. It had no roof, was open to the sky—and it
must be uncomfortable and difficult when it rains or snows.
But Chinese women wear only simple cotton underpants, no
tights, girdles, stockings or slips, so perhaps it is not too complicated and awkward for them. I was relieved to be left
alone as I am not always sure which way one is supposed to
face. The girl who escorted me tactfully waited outside after
she had shown me the communal roll of toilet paper hanging on a post. Surprisingly, there were no flies.

As at the commune, we washed our hands in basins outside the house where we ate and went in to another sublime
meal, even out here where facilities are limited. A new dish
today was candied white potatoes so scalding hot that you
plunge them into ice water before putting even a tiny piece

70

in your mouth. The candied coating becomes an absolutely delicious hard caramel. To see ice surprised me, but later today in Peking I saw a wagon piled high with big hunks of it, covered with straw but dripping, nevertheless, in the terrific heat. People were buying smaller pieces that were chopped off, the way I remember ice in my childhood, and even up to World War II in Connecticut. We saw a young boy with some tied on behind the seat on his bicycle and we hoped he did not have far to go as it was melting fast.

After lunch we sat outdoors and watched an entertainment of songs and dances put on for our benefit. The Chinese musical instruments consisted of two kinds of violins that are rounder and smaller than ours; a bigger one which sounded more like a cello and looked like a barrel; and the biggest bright red drums I have ever laid eyes on. One song was called, "The Song of the Hog Breeders," others were about winnowing grain and planting rice, and all were accompanied by the now familiar energetic dances we are getting used to. They told us these were original, made up by these students, but to us they seemed pretty much like all the other dances we see everywhere we go. I wonder if they *really* are serious about a dance celebrating hog breeding; I wonder if anyone thinks it is funny or far-fetched. It is hard to believe they are all so naïve and steamed up about pigs and manure, but I suppose it is symbolic; it represents the equality of everyone and the value of all kinds of work rather than simply manure and pigs.

We saw the barracklike rooms where they sleep, eight or ten beds in rooms with big open windows, no screens and hard dirt floors. The beds are real beds, each with a plastic cover over the blankets to protect them from the dust that is everywhere. Each student's belongings were neatly piled under her bed and each had a wash basin, towel and washcloth hanging above. It is exactly like a Girl Scout camp, yet these campers are all adult, most are married. It must be an odd way to live for six months, but they all seemed content and even excited about what they were doing—learning the value of manual labor.

June 8

CHINESE CITIES are organized into Street Committees—the most grass roots personal level of government there could possibly be. It is a combination of old-fashioned New England village community life plus a highly structured family life, all mixed up together. Everyone has a role and responsibility, everyone has a sense of self-respect and of his place in life. There are twenty-five street committees in Peking and the one we visited has jurisdiction over 132 small lanes or *hutangs*. These *hutangs*, wide enough for one car, have high walls on each side, behind which are traditional Chinese courtyard houses. Constructed on the same order as the Forbidden City palaces, you go from building to building through courtyards and gardens; even in these small versions you feel they could go on forever. From the street you enter through a gate and never see the first courtyard or house straight ahead; you turn to either left or right, walk through and out of the entrance and suddenly a whole compound of houses and gardens opens up to you. The headquarters of this committee used to be a rich man's private house and I can't help but wish I had seen it when one family was living in it. Now the rooms are whitewashed and stripped of everything but the bare essentials, with no decoration except the inevitable pictures of Marx, Engels, Lenin and Stalin, four in a row on one wall, and of course, Chairman Mao on another.

There are 14,136 households comprising approximately 53,000 people who live in these 132 *hutangs*. Of these 22,808 are workers, nearly half of them women, a little over 16,000 students, 6,142 children under seven and 7,762 "pure residents," by which are meant veterans, the retired, old housewives and the disabled who cannot work. This committee is divided into five sections and run by sixty-five paid staff members. Manager of it all is a forty-seven-year-old woman whose title is Head of the Revolutionary Committee. Her salary is a little over 100 yuan, about forty-five dollars a month. She is the only woman chairman of a street committee in her district, but many women are vice-chairmen. Formerly she worked in Shanghai but was transferred here because her husband serves as a member of the Revolutionary Committee of the East District of Peking. They say that families are not separated as much as they used to be, and that they can ask to be moved, as this woman was. But when husbands and wives are apart because they have been ordered to work in different sections of the country, they are given twenty days, not counting travel time, to visit the other—twenty days out of a year to be together.

This chairman has two sons, aged nineteen and twenty-one, both of whom are in the army, and a girl, seventeen, who goes to school. She lives with her husband and daughter in a courtyard house in the East District. The boys can ask for leave to come home occasionally, but they do not get regular leave.

Under the Street Committee's jurisdiction are six factories established during the Great Leap Forward, ten primary schools, four day care and boarding nurseries where babies can be placed when they are fifty-six days old and the mother returns to work; one service center and eight service stations, which take care of the domestic chores of the workers, one very simple hospital where the medical level is not very high, but the object is prevention of disease rather than cure.

I used to think that in a Communist country everyone is a member of the Communist Party, but that is not the case. The party is an elite group and its members are chosen by the top officials and asked to join. In the Soviet Union only about 5 or 6 percent of the population are members of the Communist Party, considerably less in China. And of course, there is no other party to belong to. Party workers devote their extra time to organizing the "pure residents" into study groups and teach them about state affairs and Mao philosophy as well as practical skills, so that these people who don't have much of a worthwhile place in many societies these days, can assume an important role in the life of the Chinese cities. In fact, everything depends on them for they are the foundations on which the whole structure rests; they are responsible for the details of everyday life and so free both parents to work in "building up the country," as we hear so often. They take care of children; they shop, chop, prepare food and sometimes cook for families; they do mending and laundry in the service stations, see that shoes are repaired; they keep stoves burning and keep house keys (I wonder why they have keys if everyone is as honest as we are led to believe?). Some are in charge of sanitation and hygiene and learn to give massage and prescribe medicine and treatment for simple ailments; other groups knit or sew or do embroidery. The "pure residents" are not paid as most have husbands or children bringing in wages, or if not, they are supported by the Street Committee. The Street Committee also participates in the management of vegetable stands and coal dumps where members either buy or receive their quotas. Most of the houses in this committee were old courtyard houses, but naturally, in many districts, there are new apartment buildings.

At the entrance of the nursery is a large poster reading, "I will grow up to be a worker, a peasant or a soldier." Another advised, "Build our country on the basis of frugality." We saw the sewing and embroidery room where women were doing what we used to call piece work; sewing buttons on a finished sweater, appliquéing decorations on babies' buntings (babies' and childrens' clothes are made of bright prints and gay colors in contrast to the drab sameness of adults' pants and shirts). We saw entrances to air raid shelters in every courtyard, manholes in the ground, but we could not go inside. The reason given today was that the ventilation and other facilities are not installed yet, but no matter how often we ask, we have not been able to see a shelter. As we know of other people who have been taken on inspection tours of shelters, perhaps it has something to do with Harrison being a journalist. We also don't get anywhere each time we ask to see the subway, which is being constructed so that it can be used for a shelter, too. We visited several women in their homes, now only two or three rooms for a family and several sharing one courtyard. Previously, one family might have lived in a house with ten, fifteen or more rooms and almost as many courtyards. Vegetables grow in every yard in tiny plots and here, for the first time outside workers' houses, we saw one or two flowers, even some in pots. They certainly were a cheerful sight.

Everyone we saw looked happy and busy and I can't help

thinking what a wonderful thing it would be for our cities if we could organize our citizens into committees like this. If every individual felt a part of a neighborhood, really a part of it, and had a job and responsibility that were vital to him, and to his own little community, it could transform our cities into a series of towns and villages, safe, comfortable and human again.

Last night, with the Dudmans and one of the correspondents here we went to a Mongolian restaurant about twenty minutes from this hotel, beside a lake. On the way we saw a big rainbow reaching all the way across the sky, a perfect arch. I haven't seen one like it for ages, I doubt if a rainbow could show through the smog and dirt in New York. We sat upstairs in a room that opened onto a porch on which was a large round stove. We were given several bowls of different uncooked food, meat, greens, other things I didn't recognize. Each of us mixed up our portions, or more accurately, scrambled them with two eggs on the stove, sort of garbagy but good. The correspondent senses that there is a continuing power struggle in the Chinese government, a very deep-seated struggle.

We had a message through H.'s office that there are blue-birds nesting in our country garden. I find that hard to believe, a miracle if true. I haven't seen a bluebird since 1958. H. insists he saw one last year out on the road but I have never believed that; I think he made a mistake. We put up three houses especially built for bluebirds this spring and they are supposed to be coming back little by little to other places, so perhaps they are coming to us.

Thinking about bluebirds and home makes me long to be back there. Spring is a terrible time to be away—I feel homesick and discouraged. We have been here eleven days and still we know nothing definite about going anywhere; when and if we do go I feel sure it will be more of the same

—flour mills, factories and pig farms; nurseries and kindergartens and schools where the main courses are in the making of transistors and the study of Marx, Lenin and Mao's thoughts. There is so much wrong with our system but I am beginning to realize that there is certainly much to be desired in this. Does freedom always breed ills? Can capitalism ever be made to work for everyone? Do we have to resort to such a controlled society for all the people to be fed and employed? Can't there be a middle course? The presence of members of the Revolutionary Committee and soldiers in every establishment, even if they look like everyone else and often don't wear distinguishing clothes, is depressing. I am conscious of the lack of real freedom everywhere even though I haven't yet seen or talked to any Chinese who didn't seem cheerful and interested and fully involved in his or her life and work. But I asked our interpreter if he could leave the country if he wanted to and he answered matter-of-factly, "Of course not." Overseas Chinese can come and go and they are not urged or forced to stay here as the present government feels they would be restless under this regime. But a Chinese citizen can't go anywhere, he is a prisoner in his own country, even his town.

June 9

Still in Peking

SUPPOSEDLY we are leaving Sunday to go on a trip to Sian and Yenan. I will believe it when we get there.

This morning we went to the zoo where H. saw two real live pandas for the first time in his life. (I saw one in London in 1960.) One was very dirty and dusty, and the other was a perfect panda, big and very black and very white. He walked near us in his slow lumbering gait, sat down and posed for a photograph in a professional manner. An animal I never knew existed, the "lesser panda," is a mixture of a raccoon, fox, cat, with a panda's striped face, brown and white and a little black, very odd. We also saw the musk oxen that Nixon gave to the Chinese. They were in adjoining pens and didn't come near enough for us to get a good look at them, but all the Chinese people at the zoo got a good look at us. I have never imagined that I would be the object of such curiosity, people came right up to within an inch or two of my face and just stared, unbelievingly. I wish I could read their minds. What are they thinking of? Are we as peculiar as the mangy, straggly musk ox? Here in Peking you would think people would be used to foreigners; after all more than sixty ambassadors are now in residence and lots of foreign correspondents, many of whom have been here for some time.

Tonight we went to the ballet to see "The White Haired Girl." I loved it, it was glorious! The scenery is marvelous with changing moving backgrounds; there is a terrible wicked landlord with silk clothes and a Panama hat and the evil men who work for him and chase, torment and beat the peasants. It is the story of a peasant girl who is taken from her father because he failed to produce his quota of grain to the landlord although he had worked as hard as he could all year; there just wasn't enough. The father puts up a fight, is killed in front of his daughter, and she is taken to the landlord's house where she is forced to do heaven knows what. The old lady of the house is religious and wicked—two characteristics that often go together—and after prostrating herself and praying in front of the Buddha she jabs the girl with a long pin because she is sleepy from overwork. When life becomes more than the girl can bear, she flees, hotly pursued by men with lanterns and whips. She escapes to a cave where she lives for several years. During this time she is so frightened by wild animals and thunderstorms her hair turns white. As it changes color, several different ballerinas dance the heroine's role, disappearing and reappearing from behind the scenery, each one with lighter hair until finally the last dancer's hair is pure white. This last girl, who is not the first heroine, continues in the leading role for the second half of the ballet as the part is too strenuous for one ballerina.

The music is more like old-fashioned western music than Chinese; there were only western instruments in the orchestra, and I noticed only one girl among the musicians. The dancing consists of traditional western ballet steps with some Chinese gestures and posturing thrown in; and singing by a mixed chorus sitting in the orchestra pit is interspersed at various crucial times in the story. I can only describe the singing as harsh—it isn't like ours at all, there is no melody as we know it, no gradation, and it is all loud.

The average Chinese woman seems flat-chested but we noticed that all the ballet girls had breasts. I don't know why there should be this difference. While older Chinese women don't wear brassieres most of the young ones do, especially in the cities (the opposite of the current trend in the United States). But the average woman in the street wears a loose shirt hanging straight and her figure wouldn't show much no matter how she was endowed, while the dancers wear the traditional Chinese jacket fastening on the side and it can fit very closely.

One thing that bothers me here is the noise. Though I live in New York City and am accustomed to plenty of racket there is nothing to match the noise of this Asian city. I am sure I could never get used to it. Every sound seems sharp and penetrating, from the constant car horns to bicycle bells and people's voices. Added to these is a sort of outboard motor sound, a small gasoline engine attached to a cart that makes an amazingly loud sputtering put-put. Every morning at about five o'clock I hear a lot of these carts moving all kinds of goods along the city streets—wood, vegetables, coal briquettes, baskets, straw mats, and other supplies.

The taxi drivers keep one hand on the wheel and one on the horn. With many more bicycles and pedestrians than cars I suppose it is necessary to more or less plough the former out of the way. In the long run if they have more cars, I think they will have to divide up the streets into separate alleys for cars, bicycles and people.

The noise of children in the school rooms is ear-splitting. From two-year-olds in nursery school to adult performers in May 7th schools and on the stage, the voices are shrill, high-pitched without much shading and *loud*, louder than any voices I have ever heard.

June 10

THIS MORNING we visited a textile factory which is organized like a commune, the same as all the large factories. There are living quarters for the several thousand workers, nurseries for babies whose mothers work there, kindergartens, primary and secondary schools, their own fields for vegetables. The apartments are airy and private, most families seem to have their own toilet and kitchen, some share them with one other family. I noticed that all the apartment doors had locks and any our host knocked on, with no answer, was locked.

The factory seemed to me very efficient and was turning out a huge amount of cloth—cotton and cotton mixed with synthetics in many weights. But here, especially in the tremendous shed where the looms are located, the noise was so terrible I had to cover my one good ear. I felt even that short exposure might deafen me forever. I don't see how it can help but affect anyone who is there for several hours, and every day. The Chinese are always asking us in the most modest and disarming way to please tell them about any shortcomings we see, and generally we can't imagine suggesting anything, but we both mentioned this. They said they were experimenting with quieter machines. Of course, the shed is too large and holds too many looms so that even if they were quieter there would still be an awful noise.

This afternoon Mrs. Paynter from the Canadian embassy took us to some of the shops that have old things and we bought some pretty bowls and spoons so we can have a Chinese meal in the proper dishes at home. Nothing older than one hundred fifty years can be taken out of China now; evidently during the past few years many ancient art works were taken out, and Chiang Kai-shek carried off many treasures to Taiwan, but now the government has stopped that and realizes that the culture of their past is worth preserving. We were told that since Henry Kissinger was first here last year the prices for antiques have gone up 100 percent.

Nothing was scheduled for tonight so I watched TV again. Several times after dinner when H. has been busy I have spent the evening in the public room on this floor. The room is usually full of other guests, either Chinese or Japanese (who can generally understand and read Chinese as the characters are similar) and they always look at me as much as at the screen. I think every floor has a big room with comfortable chairs and a TV. There is no real "lounge" downstairs, only two tables and a few chairs in the entrance-lobby, that seem solely for waiting. I have seen all of "The White Haired Girl," which was easy to identify even before I'd seen it on the stage, and various programs of dancing, singing and obvious propaganda talks. Even without understanding what was being said, I found it interesting. Incidently, I have noticed that in the communes there is a TV in a public room here and there, but only one family we've

met so far has a set of their own. Their daughter is an actress
and they watch her performances.

Tomorrow, at last, at 6:00 A.M. we fly to Sian and Yenan
for five days.

June 11

On the plane to Sian

WE LEFT at seven after a terribly hot smelly night. That is the only trouble with our hotel—there is a chemical factory not too far, certainly not far enough away, and almost every night the most awful smells come blowing in our windows on the hot wind. It is too bad, for there are lots of factories in and around Peking and there seems to be no control over pollution from their smokestacks. Some smoke is black, black as you can imagine, and some is thick and yellowish.

This is a nice two-engine Russian plane, two seats on either side, only about one half full, all Chinese except us; two smiling pig-tailed stewardesses. We had glasses of tea on the first lap to Taiyuan, where we stopped for half an hour and got out and walked around and had more tea in the airport. Flying like this and making stops makes me think of traveling out west on trains in the past in the United States, getting out at the stops and walking up and down the platforms, talking to other passengers, buying a postcard or souvenir in the station. How nostalgic it makes me! I wonder if our trains will ever come back. When they used to be good they were so much more fun than flying is now, and so definite. You went to the station, bought a ticket, either checked your bags or a porter carried them onto the train for you, the train left when it was supposed to, the weather never really mattered; there was no waiting at either end, trains were usually on time. The food in those days was delicious; there never have been lamb chops as good as those on the train from Boston to New York. And the breakfasts, with so many choices of pancakes or eggs, bacon, ham. My mouth is watering remembering it all, especially since all we've had is tea and an apple and now the orange soda drink that is everywhere in China.

We are flying south and a little west of Peking and when we took off the country was fertile and green. But soon it changed to brown dusty stretches, all ploughed and, I guess, planted, but I couldn't see from this far up. There seems to be no water and I see what look like old river beds, dry now, and with trees planted in them. I can't imagine what can grow here. We passed over a rugged mountain range that looked like the Grand Canyon, red and rocky; we could see how they have smoothed the tops of many mountains and planted crops in large terraced plots. Fantastic, from here the tops seemed to have been cut off with a knife. Now we are flying over dusty arid plains with those queer signs of wind erosion, as if a giant had lain down in the sand and waved his arms, the way we used to as children in the snow. Though it looks barren, strangely there seem to be several sizable rivers and not too far from Sian we fly over the Yellow River, one of the largest in China. But the many dried up river beds certainly show what man in his ignorance has done all over the world; chopped down the forests; cleared, burned over and dug up the earth; created perfect conditions for erosion with no trees or cover to hold the soil and the moisture in it. The Chinese are planting trees along every road and have huge areas of reforestation as well as countless irrigation and flood control projects so perhaps eventually they can make their whole country green and fertile, even in the deserts. The Yellow River was known as China's sorrow because until recently there were terrible floods; millions were made homeless or swept away every year. But now, thanks to a system of dikes and dams and canals, the raging water can be regulated and used.

June 12

Sian

SITUATED IN A fertile basin between two rivers and south of a third, Sian was the capital of the empire for nearly a thousand years—through the Tang dynasty which ended in A.D. 907. Sian means "western peace" and perhaps it is significant that most of the diplomats in Peking have been brought here recently to see the ancient relics that have been discovered since 1968. It is now the capital of Shensi province.

At the station we were met by two men, one from the provincial government, the other the editor of the local newspaper. Driving through Sian my first impressions are of a far more provincial city than Peking. Most buildings are low and made of mud as are most walls. Everyone stares at us. The children look afraid. There are many pedibikes and men and women pulling terribly heavy loads in the city streets. Always two policemen, sometimes three, are posted at intersections; one stands on the platform and waves signals in a graceful way while the other, or others, see to bicycles and pedestrians and call instructions through megaphones. They wear white tunics, darkish blue trousers, red belts, helmets, carry a baton and wave it to direct the traffic.

Our hotel, which is absolutely huge, is made of stone, not mud, looks more Russian than Chinese, and consists of several separate buildings beside or behind each other. In our room there are marks on the wall where a picture and probably a banner have been taken down. Red stains on the wall makes us think a banner was glued there. We understand that Chairman Mao has asked that the cult of him, meaning statues, pictures, posters and slogans, be curtailed and soft pedaled. We see very few of those big white statues, and as I have already mentioned, we hear much less talk about him than we had imagined and, so far, have seen only one Little Red Book outside of a bookstore.

We have a suite of two rooms and bath and thank heaven there is an electric fan. I can't understand why those wonderful ceiling fans aren't installed in every room, especially in the new buildings; they are by far the most effective and don't blow your hair around the way the other fans do.

We had a good lunch in the dining room. A group of young people who looked nice but terribly sloppy were sitting near us and we thought they were Americans but they turned out to be Danes. I know it is the fashion for the young to look awful these days, but bare arms, low necks, very short skirts or skin-tight pants on visiting girls, and sleeveless undershirts and raveled raggedy pants on men are not appropriate or polite in a country where everyone, though monotonously dressed alike, is clean and neat and exceedingly modest.

After lunch we went for a drive to the Big Goose Pagoda. There are many legends about this and it is difficult to figure out the facts. A temple was built here in the sixth century; it was destroyed and another was erected by an emperor in honor of his mother. He is supposed to have turned toward the temple each morning and evening to say his filial prayers. In 652 a pilgrim, Xuan Zang, stayed here to translate the works of Buddha and he built the first pagoda, of five stories, to house the texts. Over the years the temples have disappeared and the pagoda has been in varying states of collapse, rebuilding and reconstruction. What we see today is largely restoration since Liberation. It now has seven stories and a staircase inside so anyone with enough stamina, which I miraculously summoned, can get to the top. On the way up on each landing you can see out the four sides over the countryside, see the ancient gates to the oldest part of the city and wall. Unfortunately you can also see many factory smokestacks which spoil the historic aspect of this ancient city. Sian is one of the most important cities of development since Liberation and has many factories on the outskirts, all giving out quantities of smoke, I may add.

The pagoda is huge, each side at the base is 148 feet long and the seven stories rise up from that. A platform and wall around it make it seem even bigger. A lovely formal garden to the south reminds me of the Palace gardens at Williamsburg—these are new according to our guide, designed for "the people." Many Chinese were enjoying a holiday here and it was a red-letter day for all because of us; a much more exciting and stranger sight than an old Buddhist pagoda.

At the museum we encountered more of the archeological finds shown in the movie in Peking. Marvelous pottery and all sorts of stone implements. It is here that they uncovered a village built in 6000 B.C. The excavation is well along and you can see the precise plan of the village, the shapes of the houses, the entrances, all preserved under a sprawling shedlike building. The authorities believe there is much more to be uncovered but at the moment no digging is going on.

This morning we visited the Sian Ballet School in a big rambling building where most of the dancers live. They don't begin studying as young as our dancers do, twelve or a little older is the usual age to start, and I don't think they dance as long because one teacher who is only in her early thirties is an ex-dancer. They were amazed when we told them about Ulanova dancing until she was fifty, and Margot Fonteyn, one of the most beautiful and skillful ballerinas in the world, who is still dancing at the same age. They know nothing of western ballets or dancers and are not really familiar with the dancing of their sister socialist states, Cambodia, Albania, North Korea and North Vietnam.

After the usual meeting for tea and introductions we watched several classes—girls practicing ballet steps, men and boys who were doing some wonderful Chinese acrobatics and operatic gestures in their routines. Later they gave us a performance of the first part of "The Red Detachment of Women," which we have not seen either on the stage or on TV. Another dance portrayed two Mongolian teen-age shepherdesses who get caught in a blizzard and in spite of getting separated, temporarily snow-blind, frostbitten, and hurting an ankle, manage heroicly to save the sheep.

Obviously this is one of the current revolutionary dances. The kindergarten children at the generator factory in Peking performed the same dance for us, and I also read the identical story as an "authentic" news item in the English language paper for foreigners, except that in the news story the girls were Tibetan. This I find ridiculous; it undermines the Chinese credibility and is so unnecessary. Perhaps the ballet is based on a real event but I don't believe the exact episode occurs in every autonomous district. They shouldn't pretend it does and expect anyone to believe it, especially after seeing this dance.

We had a very satisfactory talk with a group from the orchestra and some of the older dancers. Most of the girls are very pretty and have the same air most ballerinas have, though they look more wholesome; most are about twenty-three or twenty-four. They all said they did not want to get married until they were at least thirty-five, that they thought marriage and children would interfere with their careers. They all admitted to having a special boyfriend either in the orchestra or in some way connected to the dance group, but how much they see each other and if they ever see each other alone, is something we couldn't find out without being rude and too nosy. (We never see any signs of affection between men and women of any age; only between girls, between boys, between parents and grandparents and their children. The Chinese appear terribly reserved.)

This ballet group tours the province entertaining the people, and the dancers, like the other city people, go regularly to the countryside to get to know the peasants and the simple life. I asked a violinist what they did about their hands if they went to plant vegetables and take care of pigs and shovel manure. He said the purpose of going out to the farms is to integrate with the peasants, get to know them and how they live, not to learn how to be farmers. So musicians practice their instruments, play to the peasants, don't do manual work and take care of their hands.

Back at the hotel we ran into a diplomatic group, a whole bus full just back from Yenan. One ambassador told us he had asked the dance company he visited why they picked the ballet form when it is the most old-fashioned of all dance forms in the West and dying out in some places. He suggested that some of the newer dance forms would be more suitable for revolutionary subjects than classical ballet. Mao tells

93

them to learn the best from the West and adapt it to their own uses, and he felt they had not picked the best for their use in this case. They were nonplussed, had no sensible answer, as they don't really know anything about any other dancing. I fancy they know ballet because of their past relationship with Russia.

3:30 P.M.

We are waiting to take the plane to Yenan where the Long March ended in October 1935 (the fifteen-hundred-mile march on which Mao, accompanied by Chou En-lai, Lin Piao, and other leaders of the early Communist movement, led his followers to remote northwest China, fleeing from Chiang Kai-shek and the Nationalist armies). The air strip is small and it is very important that the wind and weather are just right, so we have been in the hotel since 11:30—four hours in which we could have been doing and seeing something else.

On the plane

We finally took off at 5:15. Met the well-known author Han Suyin in the airport, just back from a trip to the desert where she slept on the ground and washed in a tiny basin. She says eighty-five thousand people have planted several million trees in the desert. She looked marvelous in a tan silk shirt and pink trousers, Chinese black cloth shoes. She said we looked nice too—I guess because we were dressed appropriately in pants and shirts.

From the air you see that China is dotted with villages, fairly close to each other and surrounded by cultivated fields, stands of trees and tree-lined roads. Each district is supposed to be self-sufficient; the neighboring towns and counties house the factories that produce what the villagers use. It is evidently a workable system of decentralized in-

94

dustry. We notice several reservoirs, and around them the green makes such a contrast to the desert landscape. Ninety percent of what we are looking at has been planted since Liberation.

We are just about to land at Yenan and the valley is a beautiful long green oasis in this yellow country. It seemed to appear suddenly on the south bank of the Yen where the river makes a right angle turn to the north. Looking at the mountains we have just flown over I can't imagine how anyone survived the Long March, walking up and down, over and around and through these mountains and valleys.

Monday night

This hotel reminds me of the stark hotels in Russia and Mongolia. No rugs, tiles coming loose so you trip in the bathroom, the toilet doesn't work unless you pull something inside the tank each time you flush it, and the furniture is ugly wood, varnished a light oak color. Paper-thin mattresses, and pillows as hard as rocks seem to guarantee a poor night's sleep. We have three single beds and several chairs and tables; our room is right over the front door, one flight up, and it is hot, windy and dusty.

The newspaperman from Sian, who is uncommunicative and seems ill, accompanied us on the plane, and when we arrived here a smiling young member of the local Revolutionary Committee met us at the airport. Two cars were waiting for us. Our regular interpreter sat in back with us, the new man got in front with the driver. Our host from Sian had the second car to himself and I noticed that he sat in back, not up with the driver, which seemed to me a capitalist gesture. As soon as we got to our room and before we even had time to wash up, our local host led us to a dreary dining room with three big round tables but only two places set at one. The tablecloth was covered with greasy spots; it

95

was hot and airless and we ate in solitude behind closed doors. Harrison can be cheerful under circumstances like these but I get very irritated and cross. I don't like to be rushed and I feel we have a right to some personal desires even if we are visiting someone else's country. Anyway, we said afterward that we didn't want to eat there again and I, for one, will refuse to do so. This is the first time something stupid and vaguely unpleasant, really not understandable, has been inflicted on us, not eating alone with H. but being hustled to such a depressing place without a chance to wash or freshen up, as if we had done something bad and were being punished for it. Realistically, I suppose they think we want to be alone and not eat with the masses, who knows? But we never eat with the masses because they don't seem to want to eat with us. In most dining rooms, tables are curtained off from each other in what seems to me an unfriendly fashion.

Our Danish friends are here and after dinner we watched an old movie about guerrilla warfare and village people fighting the Japanese with land mines and, of course, outwitting them in the end. We can laugh, but after all, this has always been their history, fighting some invader or warlord for centuries. Its theme is naïve, like our old wild west movies, good guys against bad guys, the good guys obviously winning, but it seemed real and convincing to me just the same.

June 13

Yenan

I WAS AWAKENED at six by a bed-shaking explosion (artillery fire? blasting?) and there were several previous blasts during the night that also woke me. H. thinks they must be blasting deep tunnels, air raid shelters for the underground life they are preparing for. (In October a group of American journalists was told that shelters exist that can hold 80 percent of the population in time of crisis.)

They instructed us to be ready at eight for a tour of the Revolutionary Museum, which is a monument to Chairman Mao. It was a pretty heavy dose and not all that interesting to me—mostly photographs of Mao in various stages of his life and mementos of the revolution: cases of improvised weapons, handmade bombs, grenades, mines, (like those in the movie last night); cases of tools, axes, sickles; cases of the kinds of food Mao and his friends ate, such as millet in dishes; and the little white horse Mao rode was stuffed and displayed in a big glass case. Overshadowing everything else are the signs and slogans which the guide explained in a detailed and worshipful manner. I found my mind wandering back to my personal life as I heard 1934 mentioned, the year I was first married; 1936, the year my first baby was born, what I was doing, where living and so forth. I even remembered a special dress I had. We were interested that there was no mention of General Marshall who tried so hard to get the Communists and Chiang Kai-shek to negotiate their differences; the only American mentioned was Anna Louise Strong, whose life was so intimately connected with the Chinese Communist Party.

In the afternoon we had a tour of the caves where Mao lived during the years he spent here, the same kind in which many people still live. They are extraordinary, cut into the sides of the hills with beautiful doors and woodwork on the windows, which are covered with heavy paper instead of glass. I noticed that they are building new caves and that seems sensible to me; they are much better suited to life in this climate than the big hotel we are in. Built into the stone, the rooms keep cool in summer and retain the heat of the stoves in the winter. Usually each cave has two or three rooms, and a *kang* bed with a stove to warm it. Mao stayed in several different caves—I can't see why he moved so many times within the same area. Each of his former caves contains the furniture he used, described reverently as *his* bed, *his* desk, *his* chair, usually a simple deck chair with canvas slung between wood, and some really pretty white pottery teapots and cups, earthy and natural, much better looking than anything contemporary we have seen so far. I asked about them; they are copies of what was used in those days but they are not made anymore and there are none for sale. Too bad. The famous Chinese skill for making beautiful things undoubtedly still exists, but there is obviously no urge to create something simply because it is beautiful; everything must serve the people so any cup will do. But I don't see why it can't be a work of art and serve the people just as well.

Simple one-story houses and shops line the streets but a new four- or five-story hotel is being built of red brick and a huge new museum has been started. The present one seems big enough to me and it's hard to believe that they can add more revolutionary exhibits to the collection they already have. The site of the Military Commission, headquarters of the Eighth Route Army, is a handsome building of traditional Chinese design with a fantastic roof constructed in the most intricate arrangement of poles and cross-beams made of beautiful natural wood. While many of the caves were bombed and have been rebuilt, this building somehow survived both Japanese and Kuomintang attack. The Yenan Pagoda on a hill across the river is a symbol of the Revolution and probably many Americans have seen pictures of it. We drove up to get a bird's eye view and saw the usual smoke from factory chimneys hanging heavily over the city.

Slogans of the Revolution are all over the place here—on big red signs and posters, encouraging the people to, "Work with our own hands and we will have abundant production," "Use our own hands and engage in productive movement," and advising them that "Difficulties are not unsurmountable monsters; if everyone takes a hand all difficulties can be overcome," this last a quote from Chairman Mao.

In the evening we watched an entertainment of dancing and singing in a big theater. It was full when we arrived, only the front row seats, big soft chairs, were not occupied. Tables with cups and glasses stood in front of the first row for important guests to refresh themselves with tea or orange soda during the performance. The Danish young people were in the third row; in the second were the Filipino camera crew we have run into a few times, and some American

Chinese who are at the hotel; we were ushered to the two end seats in the front row. As we walked in a door near the stage the entire audience rose and clapped. We got to our seats as fast as we could and sank down in embarrassment; I could never get used to being so conspicuous. Soon after us the really important guests arrived, first the North Korean ambassador, then some North Vietnamese followed by the most important of all, several large dark men from Iraq. As they walked to their seats, we joined the rest of the audience and rose and clapped. After the performance we left in the proper order, the reverse of coming in, and drove back to the hotel also in that order. I am surprised that a Communist society should pay so much attention to this sort of protocol—status, really; it seems silly, inappropriate and very out of whack.

The show was like a vaudeville show of the twenties and awfully good. The orchestra played folk music with native bamboo flutes, horns like trumpets, and a wind instrument with many small pipes that sounds like a bagpipe. The dance routines were the same ones we saw in the ballet school in Sian and are evidently used in all their dances. The dancers weren't especially talented but their spirit and enthusiasm carried them through. The audience was appreciative and clapped after each dance or song which hasn't been the case at other performances. Usually, they have just clapped at the end. There is no spontaneous enthusiasm here the way there is in the Soviet Union, for instance, where people rush to the stage and have to be restrained from jumping up on it; or they will throw bouquets and shout their praises and adulation for hours. Nor is any special notice given to an individual Chinese performer—the group, the whole, is applauded. The audience was composed of workers and soldiers; I doubt that peasants from the nearby countryside come into town for entertainment. I had the impression that the dance groups go to them. I know they have portable scenery and costumes that are easy to carry. And the peasants work so long in the fields at this time of year they probably don't have the energy to do anything but go to bed after a day's work.

June 14

Sian, noon

JUST ARRIVED BACK in a DC 3 with the North Vietnamese and North Koreans. We did not exchange any greeting, in fact the Vietnamese never glanced our way as if on purpose, and only once did one of the Koreans look curiously at us. I smiled feebly but his expression did not change.

Before we left Yenan this morning we made a flying trip to a commune about half an hour from the city. This commune, which Jan Myrdal described and his wife photographed in *Life in a Chinese Village*, is much poorer than the one we visited outside Peking. We noticed there were many more children at home with grandmothers and more children per family; one couple had seven. The incomes are smaller and most people live in caves like those we have seen, rows of them, about ten doors in a row. New ones are being built using the old style windows that are so pretty. We had been told by an American visitor that no one made windows and doors like this anymore but she was wrong.

102

We stopped at the flour mill, a small operation but it processes all the grain the people use here, and we walked through an extensive orchard. The earth is so dry I don't see how anything grows especially up on the hills where there is no irrigation. But the fruit trees were thriving and the fields below looked luxuriant. As we hear almost everywhere, this is a year of bumper crops.

After lunch

Suddenly all plans have changed; we will take the train back to Peking tonight, after a banquet with the local big shots, because we must be there by six tomorrow evening and the airplane is not reliable. We have no idea why this sudden shift; Harrison is hoping it means dinner with some-one important, meaning Chou En-lai, but I keep thinking maybe Mao is sick or dead, or maybe war has been declared with Russia. Anyway, I am thrilled at the idea of going by overnight train; I was afraid our traveling would be all by air.

For our last hours in Sian a visit to another revolutionary museum was scheduled as supposedly there was not enough time to go out to Li Shan hill and the Palace of Glorious Purity, the scene of the famous Sian incident when Chiang Kai-shek was captured by the young Marshal in December 1936. But we prevailed and in the broiling midday heat we drove out, Harrison and I, our interpreter and our newspaper editor-host all in one car for a change. I asked if any of them had ever heard of the song Noel Coward used to sing, "Mad dogs and Englishmen go out in the midday sun." No one had.

It is so much more interesting to get out into the country than be whisked to revolutionary museums. To us they are really all the same. Even a skeptic must recognize what enormous strides have been made in twenty years and, knowing that, it gives me much more sense of everyday life to see people in the fields, on the doorsteps, with their children and families. We went through several villages of one-story picturesque clay houses built in traditional Chinese architectural style with turned up roofs. The clay is so hard here that it can be used for walls and building. It is mixed with water and packed down in frames; these are removed when it has dried, leaving walls that look like yellow cement and are just as hard. It keeps heat out in summer and in winter provides perfect insulation.

Long before Christ, kings used to come to Li Shan hill to bathe in the hot spring water that rises naturally from this hill. Palaces were built and rebuilt, trees planted and gardens laid out by many rulers; however, through the centuries the buildings collapsed or were abandoned. Legends of kings and beautiful concubines are numerous, but for contemporary Chinese the capture of Chiang Kai-shek is what makes this place interesting. During the Republic a watering place was established once again and Chiang was taking the baths here when he was kidnapped.

Because it was so terribly hot, we drove in the car up to the place where Chiang was actually caught. A small classical pavilion has been built on the spot, directly above the Palace of Glorious Purity, the name first given a palace built here in A.D. 747. From the pavilion you get a superb view looking out over the plains with rows of poplars and cypress; strangely it made me think of the view from the Villa d'Este outside Rome.

We walked slowly down through the smaller temples and pagodas, through gates and over little bridges to the main palaces grouped around a pond surrounded by tall weeping willows. Gleefully, our guides showed us the exact room where Chiang had been sleeping when surprised by his captors, the window he escaped from, and of course we were led

104

down the path on which his servant had helped him until they were overtaken. With malicious delight they told us he had lost his false teeth in his flight.

In one of the smaller buildings we took a bath in the emperor's tub, big enough for several people, and H. and I floated around in the hot mineral waters, then rested in a bedroom. At first I felt weak and hotter from being in hot water in such heat, but was soon quite refreshed, and after about seven more cups of tea was completely restored.

Back at the hotel we had a banquet of many courses—most were delicious. The menu included first a cold plate of meat slices, dried fish, vegetables, pickled cucumbers, tomatoes, old eggs, black from being put in lime juice; hot weak rice wine, sweet red wine, *mao tai*, beer, real ice water which we haven't had before, and the everyday orange pop. Southern fried chicken legs, mushrooms and beans, Yellow River carp—very bony like shad—shrimp and peas, beef slices in red sauce, goulash in ginger. A new taste for me was sea slugs, which were in the soup; they felt and tasted just like mushrooms.

The meal continued with two sweet cakes, one pink and round, the other sticky rice. When I thought we were all finished, a large wooden steam cooker was brought in, filled with *Jiao-tse*, what we call ravioli, and my heart sank as I don't like any I have tasted in this part of the world. It is a favorite Asian dish and can have many, or any, concoctions for filling, some I prefer not to remember. I have eaten it in Mongolia; in Sikkim and in Siberia, and had a hard time being polite in all three countries. (Italians insist that Marco Polo brought ravioli to China, but the Chinese claim he carried *Jiao-tse* back to Italy, which seems more likely.) But these were small and delicious and we were only given two each, one filled with meat and the other with vegetables. Our host said it was an old tradition to serve *Jiao-tse* when

105

there was a family reunion, which was a nice friendly gesture.

All during this meal we had bread and butter on butter plates. Pink ice cream (another first here) followed the Jiao-tse and, in spite of the fans, melted almost before we could eat it, as did the butter. We each had a pool on our plates, reminding me of the tigers in "Little Black Sambo."

June 14 and 15

On train

THIS MORNING on this train, we had a western breakfast; eggs, bacon, toast, jam, and coffee with hot sweetened milk served in another glass, difficult to pour without spilling. But it doesn't seem to matter how much you spill, everyone does, and often after a dinner, the tablecloth is just covered with food and spots.

Before each meal the cook comes to ask what we would like, and though we preferred a western breakfast, we said we would leave lunch up to him. It turned out to be one of the best meals we've had anywhere with many of the dishes we particularly like cooked superbly, especially several mixtures of chicken and peanuts, chicken and onions, chicken with green peppers, ending with canned pineapple that tastes almost fresh. I think I have gained some weight, which isn't surprising, and the other night I dreamed that two Chinese doctors were examining my stomach. One of them said, "It's all fat," and the other replied, "I'd like to see ten pounds off of here."

We have been the only people in the dining car during our meals; they tell us to come in when everyone else has finished and gone. And Yao Wei has eaten with us at both meals. Most passengers get out at the stations and buy their food from a generally large assortment sold on carts and stands—cooked chicken, eggs, fruit, huge round buns, and always, popsicles. These are sold everywhere, on streets, at theaters and in parks. During the intermission when we saw "The White Haired Girl," popsicles were sold in the lobby. People pushed and shoved so our interpreter warned me not to even attempt to buy one—I might get hurt. Even he, six feet tall, had trouble elbowing through the mob, but he finally emerged, triumphantly holding three popsicles high above his head. On this trip I licked a pale green popsicle, instinctively supposing it was lime flavor, but it was made out of beans, and surprisingly good. Also at most stations there is a long trough with several faucets, and men and women rush out of the train and wash furiously during the brief stops.

For nearly twenty-four hours we have been looking out the windows at the land, some of which we have already flown over, mile after mile of flat, flat stretches, every inch planted with crops, trees, or the bush they use to hold the soil; yellow ripened wheat in various stages, cut and stacked, waiting to be cut, or already cut and the stubble left, soon to be turned under and another crop planted, probably corn or sweet potatoes. Outside many villages huge stacks of straw enclose a flat place to thresh and dry and bag the grain. I see people shoveling it in regular rhythmic movements, like the movements in their dances. So here is an illustrated fact; their culture, the poetry and music, the operas and ballets, must reflect and glorify "the people," the peasant, the worker and the soldier, and here I am seeing it out of the train windows with my own eyes.

108

June 16

Hotel Chien Men, Peking

THE|DUDMANS are here, too, brought back from their trip to the Northeast, and they have no idea why, either. H. just called the Information Office and was told there will be an announcement soon—we are not to leave the hotel, if we have to for any reason, we must leave word where we can be reached. H. also called the Canadian Embassy, the ambassador is out of town and no one knows anything. We haven't heard from our interpreter, which is odd, as it's already ten thirty and we usually see him or have a call by eight. H. is much more impatient than I am about this and in desperation is having his hair cut—it also needs it, and this is a good time. I am sitting behind him in the hotel barber shop feeling like my mother back in the days when I was taken to the men's barber shop in the Hotel Vendome in Boston. She always watched carefully, the way I am now watching H., to be sure no clippers were used and my hair was not cut too severely. A pretty girl is cutting H.'s hair, with scissors only, and doing a very nice job. At home it always comes out too short for my taste.

This is a modern barber shop/beauty parlor combined— three chairs made in China that go up and down and back, two sinks for shampoos, one with a tray to lean back on, exactly the way we do at home; two hair dryers from Helene Curtis Industries, Los Angeles; plastic rollers, and all the equipment we use in the West; bottles of hair lotion, oil, shampoo—all Chinese products, some by Maxam which also makes toothpaste; scissors made in Germany. Chinese men and boys have their hair cut short, no hippies or eccentrics here, and Chinese women have two styles, braids or the straight, short bob, a real bowl cut. They may have it cut at the barber shop, but all the other equipment is for the visitor.

Now Harrison's cut is finished, very nice, and the girl is combing and smoothing it with a hand dryer that must have steam in it as the unruly pieces of hair are responding and lying flat. The cut cost forty *feng*, about twenty cents.

3:00 P.M.

The suspense is over, at least partially. No one is dead, war has not been declared, none of the drastic things I have been contemplating. The Foreign Office called and said "probably the Premier will meet with his American friends later on for discussion and then dinner." So here we wait, the Dudmans, the Fairbanks, Jeremy Stone and his wife (son of I.F. Stone and head of the American scientific group that is visiting here) Jerry Cohen, professor of Chinese Law at Harvard, each in his own hotel room. We are supposed to get another call around five or six. This is such a nonegalitarian way to do anything. I don't think the members of a government in the West, even the heads of state, would make such a production of dinner and get foreign visitors back from miles away, keep them waiting in hotel rooms for hours and not say what was going to happen, where and when.

10:30 P.M.

Mr. Ma came to get us at about 6:30. We had been waiting all day and though we had been told about dinner with the great man, we didn't know what time. I got myself ready except for my outside clothes at 4:30 just to be safe, and H. was all dressed by five.

We drove in a car with Mr. Ma and the Dudmans followed in another. At the huge west entrance to the huge Great Hall of the People we got out onto the enormous steps and waited a few minutes for the other American guests to arrive. Professors Fairbank and Cohen were the number-one guests, next the scientist, then the journalists. We went through the door in that order. Just inside was the receiving line, first the Premier and his interpreter, Nancy Tang; next the Vice Minister of Foreign Affairs, Chiao Kuang-hua; Vice Minister of Foreign Affairs, Chang Wen-ching; Ko Pai-nin, former ambassador to Denmark; Chou Pei-yuan, Vice Chairman Revolutionary Committee at Peking University; Mrs. Chou Pei-yuan, and others. As H. walked through the door, Chou En-lai recognized him immediately, said he was sorry it had taken so long for Harrison to get to China, he knew he had wanted to come for a long time, and shook his hand extra hard. He then led us to a stand placed in front of a large three-dimensional background picture for a photograph. Mr. Ma whispered to us to go in the second row as we weren't as important as the academic people, but the result was we got right behind the Premier in the center of the picture. Chou En-lai has many "working dinners," as the diplomats call them, and I believe guests are always photographed with him on this stand. Almost every day in

111

the Chinese newspaper we see a picture of important visitors grouped around the Premier. Perhaps we'll make the paper tomorrow. (We did.)

After the photograph Chou En-lai led the way to a tremendous square reception room where we sat in wicker armchairs in a semicircle for about an hour of tea and talk. Tables placed between the chairs held teacups with covers, cigarettes, matches and ash trays, pads of paper, four black pencils with erasers and one red one, all freshly sharpened. The tea was green and the best I have had here. Chou En-lai sat in the middle with John Fairbank beside him, then Wilma Fairbank, the Stones, Jerry Cohen, the Dudmans and us. On his other side was Nancy Tang and the other Chinese. In a row behind were more interpreters and Mr. Ma and Mr. Tang, the Fairbank's constant companion.

A beige carpet covered the entire floor. Large clusters of lights hung from the ceiling, which was carved and painted in the traditional squares, like the ceilings in the palaces; these were pale green and gold with light red accents. Single lights enclosed in glass ran all around the edge of the ceiling. The woodwork was light brown and shiny, and a mammoth picture of mountains hung opposite the door behind Chou and the Fairbanks.

The Premier managed the conversation with great skill. The first remarks were about smoking as none of the Americans smoked and most Chinese smoke constantly. He said he knew that on each package of American cigarettes there is a warning that they are dangerous to the health but that he understood people smoked just as much as ever. He suggested to Jeremy Stone that we exchange scientists to explore this, and cancer in general. Then there was some talk about combining theory and practice and how difficult it is and how well Mao manages to live up to this—one of his most important maxims. He remarked to Prof. Cohen that he had been sorry to learn that Mrs. Cohen had had to go home to take care of the children, no one else could be found. This doesn't happen in China, he said. There is always someone to help or someplace to leave them so mothers can be free.

Dick Dudman asked him what he was going to say to Henry Kissinger when he comes here Monday, June 29, but he never answered that directly. I was dying to suggest my idea—that the Chinese kidnap him, seeing that the Berrigans' so-called plot had failed, and hold him until Nixon ends the Vietnam war, but I figured it wasn't exactly appropriate. John Fairbank made a very nice statement to the effect that we appreciated being asked to visit China when our government is carrying on such a savage war so near. There was a long exchange about the Korean war. Chou recalled that an American general had said it was "the wrong war in the wrong place at the wrong time," and he praised Eisenhower for having had the courage to go to Korea and stop it. He also mentioned that after World War II MacArthur had said that the United States ought never to fight another war on the Asian continent (a dictum our present generals seem to have forgotten), and quoted an old Chinese proverb to the effect that "when a man approaches death he speaks good words." He remembered that American generals were against the Korean war and wondered why they weren't being more outspoken against the Vietnam war. Someone said General Gavin was, as well as a former commandant of the Marine Corps, General David Sharp. Harrison suggested that the United States Army is reluctant to admit its inability to win the Vietnam war because it would be bad for army morale and the image of the army in the country. He feels one important reason why the war is prolonged is that the army would rather keep hammering away than admit defeat.

Chou said that opinion all over the world is just, i.e., the people in Indo-China want independence and want to run their own affairs, and the conviction of most of the world is behind them. The Vietnamese have never been conquered, he continued; in the past the feudal dynasties of China always had to retreat; when the French were defeated at Dienbienphu after years of war, Mendes France had the sense and courage to see they had to get out. By that time the United States was paying about 80 percent of the cost of the French war and even while we were supposedly backing the Geneva accord, John Foster Dulles, our Secretary of State, was making plans for the United States to take over the war from the French.

Chou explained that the Geneva Conference in 1954 was his first experience in international meetings and he was taken in by us and Dulles. The elections should have been held in Vietnam at that time. Had that happened, he said, there is no doubt in any one's mind that Ho would have been elected. Eisenhower wrote it in his memoirs, Anthony Eden reiterated it and added that Dulles was planning not to sign the Geneva accord although supposedly we were working for it. And it is history that Dulles prevented the elections from taking place. Until that experience Chou and the other Chinese officials had believed in international agreements, he added. Moreover, at this conference Dulles refused to shake hands with Chou En-lai (a little like Nixon refusing to see Sihanouk), an appalling act of bad manners, especially for a diplomat and a member of the government of a powerful country.

The Premier quoted many old Chinese sayings and became eloquent and emotional about the suffering of the Vietnamese people. He contrasted their suffering, their being attacked on their home land, losing everything they have—their homes, children, family, livelihood—to the suffering of the United States prisoners of war who, as pilots, came halfway around the world to bomb, burn and destroy the Vietnamese people and their land. It is very easy to understand this point of view, in fact I don't see that there is another if you look squarely and honestly at this war.

About an hour had passed when he rose and we went into another large room, the Anhwei Room (there is a room named for each province and also one for Taiwan, waiting for the day when that island is again a part of China). On an enormous round table pieces of green feathery sprengeri formed a centerpiece. This must be an Asian custom because I remember, especially in Cambodia, flowers were simply laid on the table cloth. Generally the Chinese do not have any decoration on the table because the various platters of food take up all the space, and with everyone reaching out with chopsticks to help themselves, candles and flowers would be in the way and knocked over. The only place we've seen flowers on the table was at Madame Sun's, and they were removed immediately to make way for the food. But this table was so big no one could possibly reach the middle and, except for the hors d'oeuvres, the food was passed to us, all served on individual plates.

John Fairbank sat on Chou's right, then Nancy Tang, Wilma Fairbank, Ko Pai-nin, and a group including Mr. Ma and Dick Dudman. Harrison sat almost opposite Chou En-lai in between Chiao Kuang-hua and Chou Pei-yuan, then the Stones, Mrs. Ko Pai-nin, Helen Dudman, the Fairbank's escort, me, Chang Wen-ching, Jerry Cohen and back to the Premier.

The dinner was fabulous, nine courses in all, served by men and girls wearing dark trousers and white shirts or jackets. Little dishes, placed in a circle around the table, inside our plates and glasses, held delectable hors d'oeuvres, sliced tomatoes, cucumbers in paper-thin slices, shredded bean curd, regular hard-boiled eggs, old black eggs, chicken, fish, and probably other things in dishes I could neither see nor reach. The complete menu was: hors d'eouvres, crisp rice with three delicacies (I thought this was sesame seed but it is the rice scraped from the sides and bottom of the cooking pot, fried, and chicken and other divine but unrecognizable heavenly ingredients) water green soup made from greens that grow only in West Lake, in Hangchow, crisp fried chicken and crisp fried duck, French beans with mushrooms, baked shad, puree of bean soup sweetened with almond, rice, sweet rice cakes, bread and butter and a stuffed roll, watermelon slices. We were offered red wine, *mao tai*, mineral water and orange pop to drink. Each time I write out a menu I am horrified, it seems so extended and extravagant and wasteful, but you have to remember that hours and hours go into the preparation of these meals, everything is chopped and sliced and cut into pieces just small enough to handle with chopsticks and pop into your mouth. The portions that are served are never large, and it is impossible, even for an expert, to pick up much more than a bite with chopsticks.

The conversation was on the whole academic, mainly having to do with exchange students in the United States. Toward the beginning Chou proposed a toast "to the exchange of cultural, educational and other groups, not forgetting the press," and walked around the table touching glasses with all the foreign guests. He said that in the past there had been mutual hostility between the United States and China, on our side as well as theirs, because of our position on Taiwan. We must now seize the opportunity for people to get together.

John Fairbank was eloquent in urging that a real exchange is necessary, the Chinese must come to the United States, it can't be all one way. The assembled Americans could be useful to China, he thought, and he suggested that

China send men and women to study in the United States which would increase understanding between both countries. Chou seemed worried about students from Taiwan, or, as he said, "with Taiwan passports" at Harvard and other universities. He appeared to think there might be confrontations between these two groups, and arguments as to which is the real China and who are the real Chinese. This was the only thing he said that I thought a bit silly. John Fairbank replied that he had no idea which of his students had what passport, that it isn't necessary to have a passport to study at Harvard, but, of course there were students from Taiwan, most of them on foundation scholarships. Jerry Cohen said cultural exchanges are vital and cited the extraordinary results from the Ping-Pong exchange.

The conversation went easily from one subject to another, thanks to the Premier's interest in everything, his thorough knowledge of what each guest represented, and the interpreters, especially Nancy Tang. She faltered only a couple of times, one was when Jeremy Stone while talking about ways to accomplish exchanges, said, "In our country we have a saying, 'There is more than one way to skin a cat.'" It took some explaining to get the point across. We talked about how people don't have to agree to get along, that all in the third world don't agree, and things change. Who, for instance, two years ago, would have imagined that Prince Sihanouk would be in China? Harrison asked Chou if he had had any idea that their relations with the Soviet Union would be as bad as they are at present, and he answered, "Yes." He said one reason why they didn't ask H. to come over in the beginning of our contacts was because they had all read his book *War between Russia and China* and they didn't want to invite "the anti-Soviet champion" first thing.

Chou En-lai is a wonderful host and is either very well briefed about his guests, or has informed himself about practically everything in the world, and takes time to read up on the ideas and work of each visitor. Considering the number of people he must see every day and evening, not to mention the time and effort involved in running the country, this is no mean achievement. I found him a very attractive, friendly man with charming manners and a lively and appreciative sense of humor. I don't think he looks his age of seventy-four, though some people do think so; he has practically no gray hair, is lean and healthy looking and has beautiful graceful hands. He has great style, is really chic. His clothes are like everyone else's, but his Mao jacket fits and is neat, though I noticed the buttons down the front didn't match, as if one had been sewed on at the last minute before the guests arrived. He wears a button that says "Serve the People" while the people who waited on table wore Mao buttons. Coming through this good-looking exterior is an air of strength, toughness isn't quite the right word, but it is the quality that comes from intense suffering from endurance and surviving bitter experiences for your beliefs.

It was truly a wonderful evening and I came away with the impression of an extremely sharp politician and statesman, probably the cleverest on the world scene today. And a man whose heart is in the right place and works, a trait that seems to be lacking in so many big-power people. After all, what does really count except how human beings behave with and toward each other? And the Chinese seem, at least to me, to be more interested in the welfare of their masses and more aware of the suffering in the rest of the world than do other nationalities and governments.

June 17

TONIGHT H. and I had dinner with John Fraser, an attaché of the Canadian embassy; H. had met him in Hong Kong in 1966. He lives in the awful embassy compound. I say awful because I'd hate to be stashed away in a special place, not mixed up at all with the city I'm living in, always under local police guard. However, this seems to be the trend—it makes it easier for the Chinese to have everyone together, but it definitely isolates the foreigner from the Chinese.

The compound is a large area on the way to the airport and in the short time since it was established many buildings have been put up, private houses for embassies that want them, and apartments, which many prefer. We have been to the Canadian ambassador's apartment where he lives with his family; he has an adjoining apartment for entertaining at large functions. The Peruvian ambassador is planning to have both his office and his home in the same apartment building and eventually all embassies will be confined to

119

this area.

Mr. Fraser has fixed his apartment very attractively and has some beautiful Chinese things. We had a good dinner and talked about what really goes on here. We see the achievements, and there are plenty, but we don't live here where a foreigner *never* sees a Chinese as a friend, never can go anywhere without a guide or "escort." We have heard a lot today about May 7th Schools, that many writers are in them, really being detained, the same as in a political prison, only the Chinese don't call it that.

I find it hard to equate the general health and welfare we see everywhere with the suppression that inevitably occurs when any revolutionary regime tries to establish itself. Compared to Russia, I, as a casual visitor, (which is really what I am though I don't like the term) am not conscious of spying, bugging, being followed or having our bags opened when we're out of the hotel room—all things I have experienced in the Soviet Union. Here we are just kept apart and treated differently. For instance, when we go to a park, our taxi drives right through the gate, honking wildly at the throngs of Chinese who are walking, and we get out of the car feeling very conspicuous and embarrassed and capitalistic. In many dining rooms we are screened off from the other diners, sometimes, as in Yenan, put in a dreary room by ourselves. Even foreigners who speak Chinese are prevented from having direct personal contact with any Chinese people except the guides or escorts or officials in the government. You have no real chance to talk to a man in the street, a woman in her home, a teacher by herself. Always there are members of the Revolutionary Committee, sometimes of the PLA; and at schools, Red Guards and members of the Communist Youth League, always people who can be trusted to keep things in order, people in line, to allow no one an opportunity to disagree with the party creed. Americans we know who have old Chinese friends from the past, have been able to see them, and sometimes alone, but even so they felt it would be inappropriate and painful for their friends if they tried to have an intimate, confidential talk. There was no frank discussion or exchange of ideas, no finding out what they really think about life in their country today. All the Chinese reiterate that China's way now is the only way, that the thoughts and principles of Mao Tse-tung have enabled each and everyone of them to live better, work better, achieve more, and so on.

Thinking about this is very depressing; it weighs heavily on my spirit. I can't imagine living under such circumstances. There must be another way to create a decent, healthy, secure society without stifling what we cherish as our most precious possession—freedom of speech and choice. But when I think of the wretchedness of some people in my country, why should I be free to choose and talk when so many others have no real freedom of anything? Where does the answer lie?

June 18

WE DIDN'T do much yesterday and today. H. has been writing and I have been catching up with my diary. This morning we walked in the People's Park, which is lovely. It used to be part of the Forbidden City; the walks are all paved, there are cedar trees hundreds of years old, and palace after palace. At the last big palace the doors were closed and H. said, "Well, this is the end, we can't go in." But I pushed the door open and there, all around the huge room, about fifteen games of furious Ping-Pong were in progress. In the middle of the palace stood a square table and a huge white enamel container of, I suppose, water, and cups beside it. I couldn't help but contrast the scene with the past when the emperor sat on his throne in this same room and tended to his government, or his pleasures.

We walked again through the Forbidden City, and back at the hotel John Burns of the *Toronto Globe and Mail* came for lunch. He told us that he had been called in and down by the Information Department for an article he had written about China being displeased at the North Vietnamese offensive this spring. He said he was tailed for a while and it was very uncomfortable. This is the first I've heard of this kind of thing; I thought the Chinese didn't need to bother to act this way, that they were more secure and sure of themselves.

We did a little shopping, mostly looking at the Friendship stores which are for foreigners and sell only new things, copies of old. Obviously the Chinese are as talented as ever, but craftsmen now do what they are told, and there is a mechanized feeling about everything; though done by hand, they seem mass-designed and mass-produced. And of course they are, in the thousands of factories and workshops all over the country.

H. and I have taken several walks by ourselves, and I have gone out a few times alone to take pictures of people in the street. I will never be a good photographer as I am embarrassed to snap people who obviously don't want to be photographed. It's only when I am quick and can catch a person unaware that I feel o.k. But obviously that doesn't happen often because I am so conspicuous among the Chinese, even in my everyday outfit of dark pants and a light blue shirt. No one in the hotel *seems* to pay any attention when we go out this way—I guess they realize we can't go far or do anything except look.

Fairly close to the hotel is a market. A shed is open to the sidewalk and inside are meat, dried fish, rice and other staples. Under an awning outside are bins and piles of greens, radishes, beans, cauliflower, onions, and always a big heap of cabbages. When these are not all sold by nightfall they are simply left there to be sold the next day. No one touches them. Imagine that happening in New York. If I leave anything outside our door for more than a minute it is snatched

123

away. Once I planted some white scilla in the little yard by the basement door and one spring night when the exquisite blossoms appeared they were all dug up. Later I saw them in a window down the street, and I knew who took them, but I was too timid to do anything about it. I just don't plant anything but ivy there anymore.

We have seen some interesting things on our walks, on one occasion a fight between two young men who had run into each other on their bicycles. By the time we came along the bicycles were sprawled on the street and the two were yelling and punching each other, fighting as hard as they could. A crowd assembled quickly—it doesn't take long as there are so many people around at any time of day—and almost immediately the combatants were separated. Several men in the crowd talked quietly to them, clearly "persuading" them to stop, to apologize and go their ways.

Another time we saw a man on a bicycle pulling a cart laden with coal, and as he turned the corner the cart tipped over, scattering the coal all over the street. Everyone stopped, whether on bicycles or in trucks; people with brooms appeared like magic, and in no time the coal was back in the cart. Often we see young people helping older ones across the street or offering to carry their parcels. These episodes illustrate what we have been told but have been a bit skeptical about. But now we have seen with our own eyes how brotherly people are, how they will stop to help, will try to make and keep peace.

All the courtyard houses must connect, for over and over again on our walks a child would stand in a doorway looking unbelievingly at us, then run back into the house, only to reappear as we passed another entrance down the street. About thirty children followed us from behind the walls, appearing and disappearing in doorways as we walked by.

Babies and young children often wear the most ingenious

overalls or rompers. Slit from back to front between the legs so nothing is in the way of a hurry call, children can be rushed to the gutter, or just held out, or, if they are old enough, simply squat down with no interference. They are the Chinese version of training pants.

Before I came to China I heard a lot about grandmothers, mothers-in-law, and aunts, but I never heard anyone mention a grandfather. I wondered if there were any, or perhaps if most men of that generation (mine) had died in all the fighting and wars this poor country has endured. But every evening after work, the older men come out on the streets, and almost always with their grandchildren—wheeling them, carrying them, playing with them, or just sitting on the steps holding them. It is a touching sight. Incidently, while the streets are full of people all day long and in the evening, especially when it's hot as now, by eleven o'clock everyone is home, the streets are empty. And it is safe to walk anywhere, in any city or in the country, at any time.

We haven't been to the big revolutionary museum here because it is shut, as we hear many museums are in other cities, too. The reason given is that the exhibits are being rearranged. That is true. But the reason they are being rearranged is that Lin Piao, who was Mao's chosen successor until he was accused of plotting to overthrow Mao and take control of the government himself, was ousted. Obviously all pictures and references to him are being removed. The official story is that he tried to escape to Mongolia and died in a plane crash there. There must be hundreds of pictures of him with Mao and Chou En-lai dating from The Long March, and I wonder how they eliminate him from every exhibit.

The same thing happened several years ago when Liu Shao-chi was thrown out of office. He was accused of following the Russian or revisionist line, in opposition to Mao, and of scheming to gain power. It was at this time that the Cultural Revolution began.

This official turning on and off of people's feelings and thinking must be hard to take—even for the Chinese. While they are not accustomed to individual freedom and thinking for themselves the way we are—and for centuries have taken orders and not asked questions—it must be strange to be told to believe in a man one day, and that he is a villain the next. They get this about their own people as well as about Americans and other imperialists. I puzzle over what goes through the heads of Chinese when they meet us, or whether the children ever wonder why we are here. After all, until the Ping-Pong affair, Americans were pictured as enemies and now, suddenly, we are visiting all over their country as friends.

It is like the Russians and their treatment of Stalin—first worshipping him and putting him beside Lenin in the tomb in Red Square, then in the middle of one night removing his body to an insignificant grave. Russians were expected to change their point of view about the man because the government said to. Did any Russians wonder why Stalin had changed so—especially when he was dead? Do people in Communist countries really accept anything they're told? Do the Chinese accept that Lin Piao was such a traitor? Do they think Americans are o.k. now when last year they knew we were scoundrels and children in schools played anti-American games? Can people really change their ideas so fast, and can they keep faith with a government that manipulates them like this?

At eleven tonight we are going to take a night train to Anyang and from there go to see the Red Flag Canal.

June 19

Linhsien

WE ARRIVED this morning at Anyang at about eight. Not quite such a luxurious train as the one back from Sian, but comfortable and clean and pleasant. So far, we have slept very well on Chinese trains, and no doubt it is because the road bed is in good repair and they don't go too fast. We were met by two men and breakfasted at a guest house, our interpreter eating with us which is unusual. Afterward we drove here in the Chinese equivalent of a Volkswagen bus with the two very nice and friendly men who met us. The drive was about an hour and a half and the country looked pleasantly green compared to what we've been through so far; many walnut trees. Anyang and all the roads in this area are teeming with trucks, bicycles and hundreds of carts pulled by tiny donkeys, day and night. At night when they stop to sleep both donkeys and men lie down right in the road, and in the heat of the day the drivers doze under a canopy or umbrella while the donkeys plod along unguided.

127

I noticed many boys with brooms and baskets, running out to sweep up the droppings of the donkeys as they passed by.

Here we are staying in a hostel and it's not very nice—our bathroom is grubby and the toilet and floor filthy. The group of Danish students who were at Sian are here (in spite of their sloppy dress they are pleasant and friendly); they come from various schools and colleges and are accompanied by teachers. Already they have been across Siberia on the train and from here they will go to Hong Kong, Malaysia and Thailand, not back to Denmark until October or November.

Will Rogers once said he had never met a man he didn't like. Until today I felt that way about the Chinese—we haven't come across anyone who hasn't been pleasant, friendly and helpful. But the head of the Red Flag Canal Project is a smooth, bureaucratic, oily sort of man who didn't have any of those qualities. He seemed much more interested in his own position than in this monumental achievement of the Chinese people. He told us the history of the canal and took us to the museum where maps, models and pictures explain this miracle. Two girls described the exhibits in their typical shrill enthusiastic voices. It is unfortunate that so many of the revolutionary exhibits we have been to are not as good or as interesting as they could be. Usually they are made up of photographs most of which we have already seen. It's too bad. This is a great project, but they make it boring.

Lin, which Linhsien comes from, means forest, but in spite of its name, this area for centuries has had no trees. They used to say the earth is poor, the mountains are poor, the people are poor. Before Liberation there was no water except unreliable rainfall, nothing but stones and gullies, and each year as the meager crops failed because of drought, many people were forced to leave their homes to beg in other cities. Now it has all changed, thanks to the Red Flag Canal and what the water has made possible.

After lunch and a nap we drove for about two hours to the Youth Canal which is wrapped like a snake around the side of a big mountain, more than halfway to the top. The caretaker, a young man of twenty-seven, who worked on the canal when it was being built, lives in a house below—really under—the mountain, within sight and earshot of the canal. We walked down a steep path and had tea with him; the tea and water here taste of the earth, as if some were mixed up in it. This young man has a wife who is assigned to a production brigade and lives fifty miles away with their two children, five and one. He sees her occasionally, at no definite times. His job is to be on the alert for leaks and seepage. If he finds any, he telephones to the canal headquarters and a repair crew is dispatched immediately.

The next stop was a huge dam that creates a tremendous reservoir. Twenty power stations generate electricity for the villages and factories. This part of the country is terribly rocky and it is amazing the way the stones have been cleared from the fields and used for terracing the hillsides, for building houses, walls and animal pens, for every kind of construction. In comparison, the accomplishments of New England's early settlers, clearing the fields and making their stone walls, seem like child's play.

In the pictures the Red Flag Canal looks like a new Great Wall of China running through the Taihang mountains of Northwest Honan Province; it winds around hills, over cliffs, across valleys. For ten years the people of the area dug, blasted, excavated, to build 134 tunnels and 150 aqueducts that now bring water in the 1,500 kilometers-long canal from the Chanho River in Shansi province to this formerly barren land. Tonight we watched the documentary film, some of which we had already seen in Peking, of how the people did this, a phenomenal feat. Men, women, girls, boys, swarmed like ants over the mountains, hung swinging on ropes over precipices to put dynamite in strategic places in the rocks, crawled through the earth digging tunnels, inch by inch, with their hands. The whole project is inspiring and magnificent, a monument to determination and the human spirit. To be a native here now, compared to life under the feudal landlords before Liberation, and before the dams and canals, must be heaven—no matter how dirty, dusty and poor everything may look to me. The results of just a few years have been remarkable bumper wheat crops, excellent production of vegetables, and millions of newly planted thriving trees. Small reservoirs have been built in many villages, and now there is water to drink, water to wash in, to swim in, and for irrigation, where generally in the summer there was none. Today no one is starving, no one has to beg, and no one is forced to leave his home.

June 20

Linhsien

THIS MORNING we drove over what seems to me endless country, all the same, village after village, most very poor and dilapidated, but all with enormous activity, building new houses, new pig sties, fixing the roads, digging out gutters. Occasionally we saw what I thought were root cellars—mounds of earth with large stones across the openings. I was surprised to learn they are graves. Bodies are cremated in the cities, and Maoism has taken the place of religion and ancestor worship, so they say. But I wonder if that is true out here in the countryside, where they obviously bury their dead and care for the graves.

We saw more of what we had heard about and seen yesterday, that every village now draws water from the huge project for small reservoirs and irrigation ditches where women can do their washing while the water is rushing to the fields. Everything is *so* dusty; I had never thought about it before but of course this is why so many shirts are not really white but a sort of tan off-white, a natural color from the earth in the water.

We visited the main hydroelectric plant and a big aqueduct and several power stations for controlling and directing the water. The project is gigantic; we could drive for days and not see all the dams, canals and stations. It is very fertile here now and this year's wheat crop is 10 percent bigger than last year's. The wheat is nearly all threshed and put away. The yellow straw is piled in huge rectangular or round stacks and covered with mud that hardens into a protective cover against the rain, and the grain is in the village graneries. Everything else looks green—the rice is being transplanted. I still can't get over the way they have cleared so much land of stones.

In the afternoon we visited a typical village of the People's Commune. It appeared to be a hard-working, thriving community; all the land is irrigated by fifteen pumps and eight canals. The peasants have enjoyed bumper crops for the past several years; they now have a large reserve of grain, a grain processing plant (flour mill), some tractors, and machines for husking and for rock crushing. The average income per capita has risen and they possess more worldly goods. Before Liberation no one owned bicycles or sewing machines or radios, now many have them. Many new rooms have been built, all children over seven now go to school at least through junior middle school, which means seven years of school. If they want to go on further, they must go to a city school in Anyang. There is a tailor's group in each village where they can take their own material and have it made up if they haven't a machine or the time to sew. Village shops carry necessities including the thermos jugs without which no one can exist in this country.

We visited a clinic that is run by a man who has had no

formal medical training: he is not even a "barefoot doctor," but he studied and worked with a doctor of traditional Chinese medicine and is now boning up on western medicine from books and pamphlets. He takes care of head colds, the most prevalent children's ailment, and the mild digestive disturbances that apparently occur only in summer. He gives vaccinations and inoculations using serums dispersed by the county, for smallpox, diptheria, whooping cough, measles, tetanus, polio; there is no cholera, no malaria. The adults suffer from hypertension, and cancer of the esophagus is endemic. Many doctors and scientists who are working on this problem think it may be related to a black fungus that grows on sweet potatoes when they begin to go bad. As the peasants eat a lot of these potatoes and keep them through the winter, some undoubtedly do spoil. H. says he has read of this fungus that causes cancer. Another theory is that they drink water and tea terribly hot. I did notice that the tea is much hotter than it has been anywhere else, really scalding.

This doctor, as he is called, says he gives out birth control pills and that some women are trained to insert the IUD and more are being trained, but we don't see any signs of such a program working in the countryside—there seem to be hundreds of children in every village we pass. They all say it is not a going program yet, but I'm not sure you can even call it a program at this point. Incidently, the children are healthy, if dirty. Many of the smallest wear no clothes and have sturdy, dusty bodies.

We visited two older women in their houses: one was forty-eight, the other fifty-four. Both had children and grandchildren and were obviously thrilled with the few possessions they had. Both came from the poorest of peasant families, one had been a child bride at fourteen. Both houses were clean as could be though it's impossible to keep out the earth dust. Walls are decorated with calendars and posters,

133

pictures of the contemporary ballets and operas, and always a large picture of the Chairman. The woman we visited first has fourteen in her family. All her children are married and live with their families in various houses around her. The houses all connect and use the same courtyard, which had a few flowers in pots and some corn planted in a tiny plot. This grandmother lives in two rooms, one for sleeping which she shares with two grandchildren. Her husband works in the county seat and when he comes home I suppose the grandchildren just move over. She has a bicycle, a sewing machine and a large clock, several large jugs and bins filled with flour and corn, and one huge barrel of flour, sealed so it will keep. Over one daughter's house is a loft or attic where boxes and barrels are stored. H. says this woman is like all Chinese women since the beginning of time—collecting her family around her and collecting possessions, even if on a small scale. When we mentioned to someone that the country people evidently take great pride in their possessions, and obviously stored up food and goods, he replied that the peasants' lot had been so bad for so long they still have quite a way to go to reach the same level of security as other workers now enjoy.

The oily manager gave us a dinner, complete with wine and *mao tai*, 150 or 160 proof, and hundreds of dishes, the best being peanuts and a welcome dish of plain canned pineapple. After dinner we drove the two hours back to Anyang and took the train for Wuhan, on the Yangtze and Han rivers.

June 22

Wuhan

LOOKING OUT the train windows from the time we woke up until we got here at eleven yesterday morning, we saw country so green it's hard to believe after what we have been through during the last few days. It was raining and misty; bright emerald rice paddies and many fields of vegetables, lakes, rivers, lots of natural water. The villages looked awfully pretty.

Wuhan is a city made up of three cities situated where the Yangtze and Han rivers meet; Hanyang and Wuchang incorporated into Wuhan. It is the capital of Hupeh province in the very heart of China. Because water is plentiful— thirty-nine inches of rain a year—and because the growing season is long, agriculture thrives. The northern mountains form a protective barrier against the cold and at Wuhan the temperature rarely goes below 40°F. even in the dead of winter.

The two huge rivers, canals and waterways facilitate communications, and for centuries the province has been a center for trade and culture; with added roads and railroads in this century it has also been a revolutionary center. It is an attractive city with many big old trees shading the streets and it has the busy-ness of all Asian cities.

At the station we were met by three men who accompanied us right up to our hotel living room where we had tea and discussed our Wuhan itinerary. It is interesting that no one ever suggests our seeing anything old or not related to the Revolution, Liberation, Great Leap Forward. We ask if we can go to an old temple, a pagoda, or even a museum that is not primarily revolutionary, and sometimes it can be arranged, generally not.

This hotel is lovely; we have a big living room that looks out over a green lawn over some roofs to the river. It has a sofa and several armchairs and a ceiling fan. A double bed and a single bed are in the equally large bedroom and we have a table fan for cooling—a great luxury. The bathroom is spotless and three sanitary napkins are available, along with towels and soap. It is not especially Chinese or western, but a hotel you might find in any hot cosmopolitan city.

Lunch was wonderful, the best food so far, amazingly light, and anything fried is lighter than you can believe possible. The vegetables especially are delicious and crisp, and taste as if they had just been picked. We had chicken and pea pods, eggplant, tomatoes, fish from the river, a kind of goulash, noodles, chicken soup with vermicelli, and rice. After a nap H. went off to an iron and steel factory; I stayed here, washed my hair and dried it in front of the fan.

Dinner was another delectable meal and afterward we watched movies that were set up in the dining room. We saw "The Red Detachment of Women," which I didn't like as much as "The White-Haired Girl"—too much propaganda and many too many false endings. It seemed to go on and on. We also saw a short on reforestation in this country, quite remarkable. It seems as if China had no trees, was one big desert before Liberation.

In the middle of the night I was awakened by a downpour, it sounded as if the whole world were being flooded. But the morning was clear and we visited Wuhan University of Letters and Art, Engineering and Science, started in 1913. Its curriculum is still the same, though taught with a different point of view, naturally. Letters and Arts include Chinese literature, philosophy, history, economics, "librarian science" and foreign languages, English, German, French, Russian and Japanese. The science department includes math, chemistry, physics and biology.

At present, like all schools and universities, it is recovering from the Cultural Revolution. Closed down for four years, (1966-69,) it finally opened again holding its first regular class in August 1970. In 1967 the worker's propaganda team initiated classes in Mao's Thought, largely for the benefit of the faculty and administration as the students of all universities were roaming the country, challenging the status quo of teachers, education, government, society, every aspect of Chinese life.

It is hard for me to understand the Cultural Revolution. What for instance, was everyone doing during those hectic years? Were *all* the young people on the rampage? When they say there were big debates, what does that mean? When did the fighting start and when did it go from "fist fights" to fighting with "some weapons"? What were all the teachers and administrators doing for four years? Were they all down in the country taking care of pigs and using their hands and *really* changing their thinking? What happened to the buildings, did anyone live in them? Were books destroyed? It is very baffling and maybe before we leave China I will be more clear in my mind about this very important phase in the development of the Revolution. But I wonder; several Chinese say they don't understand it either and cannot answer these questions.

Harrison was told by other sources that there was more fighting in Wuhan during those years than in any other city. We noticed a bullet hole in one of the windows at the university, in fact they showed it to us. That's one very definite characteristic I have noticed; the Chinese we have talked to are honest, unassuming and not the least bit deceitful or hypocritical, very straightforward. If they don't want to answer us they don't, but nothing else is made up to take its place. Many of us in the West have grown up with a fetish about the Orient and the strange, mysterious, exotic, even spooky, inhabitants. How different these people appear from such preconceived notions, how natural. Anyway, all the faculty and most of the administration at the university are the same as before the Cultural Revolution, most went through manual labor in the countryside to help them with their "struggle, criticism and transformation." A Chinese friend told us that the words or characters for the above sound like "dopey guy."

First we met for introductions and tea with the faculty and administration, which, as always, consists of members of the Revolutionary Committees, who seem to outnumber the professors. A beautiful woman with a soft lovely voice, a heavenly smile and the most glorious white teeth, is a member of the Committee for Revolution in Education. Even with her quiet simple manner you could tell what a fervent member of the party she is. They suggested we visit a class right away, see the campus and then return for discussion.

All Men Are Brothers, or *Water Margin,* was being discussed in the light of contemporary beliefs and social structure, in the Chinese literature class we visited. I was surprised they were studying a classic but was told that these books are being reissued now and that Chairman Mao, besides writing beautiful classical poetry, is a great reader of old Chinese literature. In the picture taken of him and President Nixon at the time of the famous visit, they are sitting in armchairs with bookshelves behind filled with classical volumes, and the tables nearby were heaped high with more books. In the classroom a diagram of the plot was on the blackboard, and the young teacher was talking with passion about class struggle; revolutionary thought; loyalty to family, mother, monarch (in the past), country; betrayal; the relationship between historical conditions and the personal role in uprisings and revolutions. All these concepts were related to the characters and themes in this great book and, of course, to present-day China.

The students looked the way all students do here, some in PLA uniforms, the rest, both young men and women, in the usual dreary clothes. They each had a copy of the book in front of them and some were taking notes, some were not.

We drove around the campus, visited several buildings, and returned to the original room for a long discussion. This room had the nicest piece of furniture I have yet seen in China—a kind of sideboard of simple waxed wood. It reminded me of early New England or Shaker furniture in its straightforward lines and soft finish, not shiny and varnished the way so much furniture is here. The chairs and sofas were upholstered in straw, with green leather (or plastic that looks like leather) trimming. In the hotel the covers are the same, only with maroon trim. Present were the beautiful member of the Revolutionary Committee in Education, professors of biology, Chinese literature (the latter had taught the young teacher we had just listened to), two students, two others from the reception section of the university. Harrison, as usual, asked them to tell us what happened during the Cultural Revolution; he is determined to get some kind of understanding of this enigma, but often the discussions don't really add up to anything we can interpret or comprehend in the light of our own standards and ideas.

While this university was closed, the professors and administration spent a great deal of time, here and in the countryside, studying Mao's Thoughts. The Cultural Revolution, they explained, changed people's thinking primarily by reasoning and persuasion though there was some fighting. The literature professor, who studied at Columbia University in New York in 1947-48, said that he had had the wrong academic outlook before the Cultural Revolution, his ideas were erroneous. For example, in *Water Margin*, formerly he would have taken the hero as he is presented, would have paid little attention to the peasant uprising, when in reality, that hero betrayed the peasants, is actually a traitor, and the peasants are the heroes. But he did recognize that they must accept their literary legacy in a literary way, pay great attention to and study the past, take what is good and criticize what is bad. According to him, very few books were burned during the Cultural Revolution, but I can't tell what that means. He also said that not many of the classics had been published as yet, that there have been too many other things to do, and that they were not widely published before. Publishing is going through struggle, criticism and transformation, and a preface will be attached to all classics and prerevolutionary books advising the reader to "Let the past serve the present."

The English language professor had two students with her, a boy and a girl. She described how formerly five years was needed for perfecting a language because they taught literature and history along with the language. This is now considered divorced from reality; the stress is on language only, as the sole object is to train interpreters and translators. Foreign languages are no longer cultural subjects, they are considered to be tools and weapons in the fight for socialism. H. kept insisting three years is not enough for a first rate interpreter, and she admitted that they can give only the fundamentals in that time.

Chinese history, past and present, and modern world history are taught, the latter including the history of the international Communist movement. A group of teachers study the United States. There was no mention of any other language classes and no teacher representing them, but foreigners in Peking have told us that the interpreters in other languages are excellent, as good as ours is in English, which is perfect.

The biology professor, sixty-four years old and a self-styled intellectual, was born and educated in the feudal and bourgeois old society. He expounded at length on his prerevolutionary errors. His thinking had been oriented in a bourgeois way, he went abroad, he studied at Edinburgh and he had a bourgeois world outlook. Before the Cultural Revolution he primarily wanted recognition for papers he wrote, wanted to discover new plants for the notoriety he would gain, fooled himself into believing he was contributing to the motherland. During his year and a half stay in the countryside he came to see how lofty are the ideas of the peasants, and to understand their selfless contribution—they work all year round to "serve the people." He used to believe the saying, "Those who do intellectual labor rule, those who do manual labor are ruled." When he first went to the country, the peasants looked up to him as an eminent professor of biology, but they soon found out that he had no idea even how to plant anything. Though he had written articles and taught biology for years, he knew only theory, nothing practical. He was the perfect example of "planting crops on the blackboard." He professed to welcome criticism from students when his teaching was "erroneous" and said that he had taken part in some of the fighting during the Cultural Revolution. At present the faculty do manual labor in the country in rotation; the university has opened—and now manages—two branches that are in reality manual labor camps. In addition two short-term training courses are given to teachers preparing for assignment to the middle schools.

Most of the students come here, as they do to all universities, after three years in the countryside, factory or army, although a few come directly from the middle schools. The overall requirements are the same; they must *want* to learn to serve the people better, they must be in good health, and, with a few exceptions, under twenty-five; they must be recommended by their superiors in their present situation; they must be finally approved in a personal interview at the university where they can be rejected for reasons of language level or physical health.

By 10:30 everyone was looking at his watch. I get the feeling that they are as weary with us burrowing in to try and find out about the Cultural Revolution, the changes we don't understand, as we are with the constant talk about erroneous ideas and workers and peasants and manual labor. The professors seem to like discussion but the members of the Revolutionary Committees seem to get bored more easily. They get terribly restless, shift in their chairs, swing their legs and feet, and smoke like chimneys.

As we were walking out, one of the professors mentioned to Harrison that he read the *New York Times* regularly, sent in by a friend. He said he found it interesting and enjoyable, then hesitated a moment and added, "But tell me, Mr. Salisbury, why are there so many typographical errors?"

After yet another delicious lunch we went for a boat ride on the Yangtze followed by one on the East Lake. It cooled off after the downpour last night and this city, known as one of the three ovens in China, was pleasantly mild and overcast. We boarded a sort of private excursion boat and chugged up the river to the big bridge that was built in 1957. Nearly a mile long, 260 feet high, with two levels, one for trains, the other for all other traffic, trucks, carts, bicycles, pedestrians, it is located near the place where Mao made his famous swim in 1966. The smoke from factory chimneys is bad but the smoke from the tugboats is unbelievable—blacker than any smoke I have ever seen. It is a busy river; many small boats ply back and forth from one side to the other and many freighters and junks carry goods from here along the connecting canals and rivers throughout China.

Around the shores of the East Lake are several attractive large houses which must have been summer places of the well-to-do. Today they are used as rest houses where "the people" can go for a vacation. Areas are roped off for swimming, boats are available, and, as everywhere, many trees have been planted.

After we got back from that life-saving interlude away from factories, schools and communes, Harrison had an argument with our host. He wants to see newspaper people and they are reported to be "too busy" to see him. H. suggested that if the Premier could find time to see him, he would think these people here could, but that had no effect. They exchanged rather heated words and I felt it must be hard for our interpreter to be in the middle of it, but perhaps he is used to this sort of occurrence; he never shows any emotion no matter what happens. This is the first time that something we requested through Peking has not been arranged for us. Perhaps they do as they please down here. However, there's another possibility: perhaps there *aren't* any newspapermen, just a plant where news put out by the government is printed. Who knows?

We were given another wonderful dinner upstairs in a room looking out on the river but our host was rigid and bureaucratic as he firmly reiterated that it is not possible for H. to see anyone from the newspaper. H. was very polite and tactful, so perhaps they'll come up with somebody tomorrow.

After dinner we watched a two-hour program given by schoolchildren. Although we had seen most of the songs and dances before, the orchestra was really good and the individual musicians amazing. A child no more than five played the xylophone remarkably, a boy not much older played an excerpt from the "Yellow River Cantata." It's too bad everything is so loud and strident because they're unquestionably talented people and can be taught to do anything, but it is all so noisy. The children were violently made up with bright red cheeks and black all around their eyes, as are all performers from kindergarten to professional, generally including the members of the orchestra. They look like clowns.

June 23

On the train from Wuhan to Changsha

AS I HAVE mentioned, great emphasis is put on health and fitness and most Chinese do "daily dozens." Often you see a group of workers outside a factory, or in a park, making the same slow-motion graceful gestures we watched the children doing at the middle school in Peking. When I am not too lazy, I do my own exercises, and this morning in the hotel, as I was stretching and bending, I looked out the window. Directly across the street, in his window, a Chinese man was doing the same. I wondered if, as he came into view, he noticed me, and I stopped for a few minutes to watch him. His eyes were not looking out. With fantastic concentration he went through the movements, and if a bomb had exploded beside him I feel sure he would have continued, undisturbed.

This morning in Wuhan, Harrison had a long talk with representatives from all the departments that run the city— housing, health, pollution in factories, sewage disposal, commerce, service centers, education—all the elements of the city except the newspaper. I wonder whether we may find out elsewhere how the various local papers are put together, whether they have any local editors and writers, or whether all the news comes directly from Peking.

Everyone was most agreeable and friendly, they had been called at the last minute and seemed anxious to tell us everything about each department. I think we could have stayed talking with them for many more hours if we hadn't had to take this train. That, too, is one of the drawbacks of traveling from one place to another so quickly; we just get warmed up, just get accustomed to the people we are with, just begin to understand something of their point of view, and we have to leave. At a discussion like this I am starting to anticipate the answers such as,

"We have no figures at the moment but are working on the problem."

"The committee for looking into wastes is investigating these problems."

"The great gains [in whatever field] are from mobilization of the masses."

"Venereal disease has been wiped out mainly because of the change in the social structure; there are no prostitutes any more."

The figures on health, infant mortality, births, deaths, etc. were very vague and despite a lot of talk about birth control, the birthrate and increase in population in the last few years is absolutely staggering. For birth control they say they use pills, IUD and sometimes operations on men and/or women; city women usually have their babies in a hospital but in the country babies are born at home. Midwives are trained and attend births in both places.

There is still some malaria in this hot wet place, and still the dread snail disease, schistosomiasis, which is spread through water and attacks the intestinal tract.

It is not clear whether the Chinese officials are concerned with the terrible smoke from the factory chimneys or the black clouds emitted by tugboats on the river. Their creed is to use any and all waste material to be sure not to lose a potential product, but I suppose they really are no different from any other country that is trying to industrialize; production and catching up with the rest of the world are what counts, the problems of pollution can wait. But that is the trouble; pollution can't wait any longer, here or anywhere else.

In Wuhan some of the sewage is piped to the countryside and some is treated and discharged into the river. As it is thoroughly treated, they say it does not pollute the river, that, as in the United States, the industrial wastes from paper and coke factories are the worst offenders. From these industrial dregs material for highways, building blocks and fertilizer can be made, also waste water and gases can be utilized. How far along any of these processes are is hard to discover. Night soil is collected daily, it is siphoned into trucks or put in wooden barrels that are pulled by men on pedibikes and carted to distribution centers where it is sent to the country, usually by boat. In the countryside it is covered with dirt and allowed to ferment before using the water in the irrigation ditches and the solids on the crops. We have been by these places near communes and they are pretty smelly. The man in charge of waste at the steel factory seems very smart, knowledgeable and aware of the whole pollution picture. He said they are experimenting with a method of desulphurizing coal right at the mine. This would do a lot to cut the pollution caused by factory smoke.

The commerce department runs the hotels and the centers that serve the everyday needs of all the people, laundries and repair shops, as well as vegetable markets and food

147

stores. We talked about the fluctuation of food prices according to the season—it occurs in this organized socialistic society as it does everywhere else, and they quoted the old saying, "As soon as you see a snowflake in the air the price of vegetables will soar up." I asked why they don't have a canning factory for fruits and vegetables but, as we have been told before, vegetables are dehydrated, salted and pickled, and some are sent to other parts of China where they don't have such a thriving agriculture.

This train, like the others we have been on here, is comfortable, spotless and cooled with fans. We have a compartment—the same as on the overnight trains—two long seats that are our beds facing each other, and two upper berths. A table covered with a white cloth is under the window. It holds a lamp with a red silk shade, an ash tray and cups with covers for tea. The girl conductor washes the floor with a mop after each big stop and in between wipes off the windows and sees that everything stays clean and fresh.

June 24

Changsha

WE ARRIVED here yesterday about 6:30 P.M. and were met by the friendliest man so far, always smiling, and with a wonderful sense of humor. Changsha, the capital of Hunan Province, lies south and a little west of Wuhan, on the Hsiang river, about forty-five miles from Lake Tungting, the second largest lake in China. Changsha means "long sand-bank" and indeed there is a long island in the middle of the river. The rain is even more plentiful than in Wuhan, often as much as seventy-eight inches yearly, and the province has always been one of the major producers of grain in the country. Rice is the main crop, also maize, wheat, sweet potatoes, soya beans, hemp, cotton, peanuts, tobacco, sugar cane, oranges, tea, rape (a kind of mustard) and tea oil. Harrison and I had never heard of tea oil, which is rare and expensive, nor of oyster oil, which we often have in sauces. Hunan province is in the middle of China and has always been an important communications center. A good system of

waterways and canals linked it to other provinces long before the railroad was built in this century.

We have two rooms in a hotel that seems less formal than
any we've stayed in—the girls yell at each other in their
high-pitched voices and the atmosphere is more casual. A
mosquito netting completely surrounds our bed and we
sleep, or at least try to, on a straw mat placed directly on a
hard base. I found the mattress leaning up against the wall
behind the bed, hidden by the netting, but it is too heavy to
move and it would be awfully hot. Obviously, that's why
they have taken it off. H. manages to sleep better than I do;
I stick to the straw and don't find it as refreshing as I
thought at first, but the only alternative is a huge bath
towel, which I think we are supposed to use as a blanket. I
tried to sleep on that but it gets all mussed up and uncomfortable under me. Once again, the dining room is divided
up into several areas by screens; we sit in one section with
some of the Filipino groups we keep running into, an American medical group occupies another section, and the end,
nearest the kitchen, seems to be reserved for the Chinese. I
don't understand this arrangement at all. It seems unfriendly and makes me feel peculiar. The food isn't as good as in
Wuhan, and the temperature and humidity are so high we
are just dripping all the time. Fortunately we have a fan in
our room and there are fans in the dining room.

This hotel is inside a high gray wall, has wings on three
sides and planting in the middle of the drive. The center
wing, which houses the dining room, looks like an old traditional Chinese structure, two stories high with a curved roof,
but it was built in the 1950s at the same time as the other
buildings. A hotel shop sells fruit, candy, a few knickknacks
and the instant coffee we had in Anyang for breakfast, a
square white lump that magically turns brown when mixed
with water and makes sweetened innocuous coffee.

Changsha is famous for its marionettes and for its shadow box plays and last night, after a quick dinner, we went to the theater to see them. Neither H. nor I had ever seen shadow box theater before and I imagine not many Americans have. Shadow plays, or shadow shows, originated hundreds of years ago in the Orient, were popular in the United States during the eighteenth century, but since have been produced only occasionally at home. Talking puppets perform on a screen of cloth or paper that is lit from behind (like the silhouettes we used to make behind a sheet). Traditionally, Chinese puppets were made of donkey skins dyed bright colors; other countries used camel and buffalo hide. I don't know what they are made of now, but they are flat and look as if they were cut out of cardboard. The screen seems to be enclosed in a small frame—or box—the whole effect something like that of an animated cartoon.

One play was about a boy who helped an old man whose cart broke down. Other people helped the boy. While the boy was helping the old man, his little sister got lost, whereupon many more people appeared to help find her. This theme seems childish and unsophisticated, but this is the way most of these people are. Everyday I see examples of one person helping another, a young boy leading an older man who is baffled by traffic; a man making sure the man next to him has tea; all kinds of little gestures, thoughtful and selfless. A second shadow play featured cranes and a tortoise—charming and very funny.

The marionettes were quite big compared to the shadow box puppets, almost half life-size, and were manipulated from below (this was demonstrated at the end). There were several skits, scenes from various Chinese operas, and some of the dances we're getting to know so well. It's remarkable that marionettes can be made to perform them so cleverly. One skit was about a United States general and three South

Vietnamese soldiers being made fools of by one young North Vietnamese man—it was real slapstick and got a huge response from the audience. I wondered if our hosts thought we might be offended, and if they cared, or if they thought about it at all. I don't think many Americans would take a Chinese guest to an anti-Chinese play.

Behind us at the theater was a group of American Chinese, about eight girls and two boys. Looking at them we couldn't tell that they weren't native Chinese except for their clothes. They were having trouble with language as they speak Cantonese, and not much of that, and the national language of China is Mandarin, which is Peking Chinese. One boy speaks both, fortunately.

Back at the hotel we went to their rooms and talked for a while. Many have relatives here, not immediate family, but aunts or uncles and cousins. Most of their relatives were pretty paranoid, didn't dare really talk, thought people were listening to them all the time—not that there is any bugging of rooms, it's just that someone is always around, hearing everything. We talked a good deal about the lack of sexual contact, or at least the lack of any overt relationship between boys and girls. We all think there isn't any sex until marriage, and marriage is put off until girls are twenty-five or so in the cities, though certainly not in the country; many country girls marry and are mothers by twenty. I said that I had not noticed the slightest sign of affection between two people of the opposite sex, only girls linking arms, boys with an arm thrown around a friend's shoulder, mothers and others kissing babies. One of them said she occasionally saw a boy and a girl walking at night with a bicycle between them and they might touch shoulders if they were really fond of each other. I have noticed couples sitting on benches in parks, and strolling, but always far apart, nothing demonstrative ever.

152

We say love will find a way, but I think Chinese young people are kept in a simple sort of girl- and boy-scout atmosphere; they do everything in a group and they are too occupied to have time to think of sex. It doesn't sound normal but there seems to be a definite playing down, a soft pedaling, of love between the sexes. Even in their most romantic ballets the real love appears to be "the cause"; the relationship between the hero and the heroine simply emphasizes it. Also, even when and if they do have the inclination, and can find time, there is no privacy. This tremendous country is a series of villages and everybody knows what everyone else is doing. Affairs are frowned on, pills and abortions are free and available, but almost without exception, both are utilized only by married women.

One girl felt the Chinese way was much better than ours, where there is so much pressure to "date" and have a boy or girl friend. Another commented that in China the whole approach to every side of life is so different. In America we talk and think so much about "finding yourself," "doing your own thing," "expressing yourself," "fulfilling yourself," etc. Here the idea is to do something for other people, the purpose of everyone's life is to "serve the people." What good is life otherwise? Only by losing yourself will you find yourself, it says in the Bible. So this is nothing new; but a chief of state teaching this and an entire population trying to follow it is new. The other day I was talking to a Chinese man about an American I knew who had killed himself, and he asked, "Why would anyone want to do that? There is so much to do for people." And yet we hear there is a certain amount of suicide, and a journalist told me that sleeping pills have a large sale here.

This morning we went to the Normal School, saw many rooms in which Chairman Mao had been a pupil, desks and chairs that he had used. Later he had taught children by day, workers at night in these classrooms. In the room where he held the night classes, several glass bulbs hung from the ceiling. These used to be just on the side; Mao suggested, and had installed an additional light that would hang in the middle. This was explained as if it were the most humanitarian, thoughtful idea, worthy of a great leader. It sounded pretty silly and exaggerated to me. We saw the well where he dashed cold water on himself every morning, then we visited a house that he had lived in. I have never known of a man who slept in so many different beds (except possibly George Washington). At Yenan there were four or five, and I believe there are more here.

This afternoon we went to the embroidery factory for which Changsha is famous. In the reception room where we sat with the director, a tiny businesslike woman, large embroidered pictures hang on the walls, depicting subjects which don't spring to my mind when I think of embroidery —portraits of Lenin and Stalin in uniform, a fiery furnace at a factory, one of the famous bridges built since Liberation, landscapes of mountains, pictures of Chairman Mao. The work is so fine you can't see the stitches even up close, and they look much more like paintings than sewing.

In the factory the workrooms are big and light and airy. We watched the seamstresses ranging from girls in their teens to older women in their sixties who have been doing beautiful embroidery all their lives and teach their special art to the younger ones. I asked about their eyes, if such fine work wasn't a strain, though I noticed many of the older women did not wear glasses, and was told that they rest their eyes fifteen minutes, morning and afternoon, out of a seven-hour day. Most of the embroidery done on silk must be for export or governmental use because it is so expensive —twenty-five dollars for a marvelous cat on an eight-inch square—or the large pictures I've mentioned or enormous paneled screens. Obviously no individual Chinese buy such luxuries and only public halls could accommodate the screens. I can't imagine how they sell all they make. The factory also produces machine-embroidered articles which, while not so delicate, are attractive and much more usable such as the pillowcases in hotels and on all the trains. We bought some and they are very pretty.

June 25

THIS MORNING at 8:00 we started off for Shao shan, where Chairman Mao was born and spent his childhood. For two hours we drove through lush, fertile land, rice paddies for miles, water buffalo, real South China landscape. On this road are still several old houses, landlord's houses, now shared by many families. I can't help but think how really gorgeous they must have been in those days.

Shao shan is a small village in a valley surrounded by hills. Many of the inhabitants are named Mao, some say as many as 60 percent. The house where the Chairman was born is down the road a bit from the village center. To get to it you walk up a path that winds past some public outbuildings, beside a pond that separates his house from that of a peasant family who have lived there for generations, and up into the front yard. Mao's family house is one story, yellow with a gray tile roof. It is obviously the house of a well-to-do peasant. There are four bedrooms; one was for the parents,

156

one for Mao, one for his brothers and another for guests. The kitchen is large, there is a separate washing room, outer rooms for tools and farm equipment, pens for pigs right next to the kitchen—handy for feeding—and a cow shed. Also a separate room for grinding rice and grain; marvelous big stones are attached to a handle that could be worked semi-automatically. The ceilings are mostly a framework of beams holding boughs and reeds under tile on the outside; parts of the house have an attic or second story. Behind the house, a few yards up the hill, is a flat mall where Mao used to thresh grain; the pond where he fished, the small plot where he tended vegetables, are pointed out with reverence and love by the guide who describes his early life.

Back in the village is the museum—a large attractive building of courtyards and covered walks with many duplicate rooms so that huge crowds can be accommodated simultaneously. The exhibits are primarily pictures of Mao's life, the history of the Revolution and Liberation, many of which we have seen. Both before and after lunch we walked through room after room, sat on tiny stools that were carried for us, and listened to explanations of the pictures, nearly dying of the heat all the while. After lunch in the huge guest house, we rested on another canopied bed in a room that was blessedly cool.

We met a group of medical people, doctors, nurses, health workers, all American. They seem terribly nice. Their organization is MCHR. Medical Care is a Human Right. I have never heard of this organization but certainly no one could deny the rightness of their motto.

Tonight we saw another performance of "The White Haired Girl." The dancers were better than those we saw in Peking but it was not so well staged and the voices were awful. Both girls were lovely and danced with feeling, and the young man was perfect, not wooden as so many of their

157

leading characters are. In the intermission we and the Filipino students and American medical group were ushered into a special room where we had tea. We talked mostly about Vietnam and how ghastly it is to be an American in Asia with our country bombing and bombing and bombing those poor people. It looks and seems even worse from here than at home.

June 26

TODAY I finally saw a landlord's house and it was a sorry
sight. We visited a commune out in the country and this old
house is the headquarters and office. It must have been very
beautiful in the days of the landlord, built beside a pond
with big trees in front; exquisitely proportioned rooms, each
one leading to another, wonderful old woodwork, stairs and
balustrades and balconies, probably teak or the dark wood
that looks like it. But it has all gone to pieces, walls whitewashed and dirty, looking like a badly kept cow barn,
woodwork broken and dull, a few windowpanes shattered,
just dirt on the stone floors. It is too bad to destroy anything
beautiful from the past no matter what the connotation. I
doubt whether any houses like this are preserved, and in a
few years they will be gone beyond recognition. Although I
am criticizing the Chinese for this, I remember many houses
left to ruin at home, beautiful big houses of another era that
no one has the imagination or interest to turn into some-

159

thing useful for the present time, so they gradually collapse while a filling station or a hot dog stand in a fake railway car, profits out in front.

Anyway, we had a nice morning there, walked for what seemed like ten miles to me in the broiling heat, ending up on the embankment of the river. There is a lot of water here and it has been harnessed by dikes and reservoirs and canals so flooding caused by heavy rain can be controlled. Before Liberation if it rained for three days there was ruinous flooding, and if it didn't rain for three days the rice dried out. But for ten years now the rice has been terrific. They have regularly had bumper first crops and this year looks as if it will be the same.

We visited the commune shop which has the prettiest blue and white china we've seen so far, made locally. The Chinese use blue and white for everyday. Also, the girl at the liquor counter said that the best selling brew is a very strong local wine, 65 proof. That's interesting as our interpreter told us that the last time he saw a man drunk was in 1958! Quite a contrast to the supposedly good neighborhood where we live in New York, where frequently I pick my way among the derelicts and passed-out bodies to get to the corner.

After lunch H. told our hosts that we would be glad to answer any questions about the United States. Unfortunately, one young man bombarded us with questions about agriculture, total rice output of the U.S., hog production, types of rice grown—which we couldn't answer. Harrison knows the wheat and corn production figures but only in bushels, which we couldn't translate into kilos or caddys in time. We'll send a *World Almanac* when we get home, then perhaps they can find all these statistics.

We drove about an hour to Hunan University after that. Here we expected the usual sitting down to boiling tea on a

160

boiling day routine, but blessedly, today we had delicious *cold* lemonade, really marvelous. The hot tea is good but it makes me perspire so that in this terrific humidity I am just dripping wet all day besides being so unbelievably hot.

We were introduced to the professors, all teachers of engineering as that's the kind of college it is, except one beautiful lady who teaches English. She went to high school and college in London, thirty years ago. I was immediately drawn to her, she seemed remote and resigned. But, of course, my reactions are very subjective—something the Chinese are advised not to be.

We visited a factory shop where they were making some sort of implement that meant nothing to me. While we were there the electricity went off, so for a few minutes it was delightfully quiet, rare in China, and we could actually hear the people talking to us. At a science laboratory they were doing something else unfathomable. At each place the lady professor said to me, "They have made a lot of the equipment, it saves a lot of money." How I would love to really talk to her, and to other Chinese who have been to other countries and universities. But probably in our lifetime that won't be possible. And, as John Fairbank said, we might as well not waste our time wishing "they were more like us." The reactions of the Chinese are not necessarily what mine would be under the same circumstances, and no circumstances I could ever find myself in would be comparable to what has happened to them in their lifetime.

H. had a long questioning bout trying to find out who picks their students, how much control the university has over who is admitted. At first they said they had a choice of applicants, but it turned out that this is the procedure: First, if a student has been through middle school and if he has subsequently spent three years in the country, factory or army, and wants to go on for further education, he must 1)

Write an application. 2) The application will be discussed by his comrades, fellow workers, squad or brigade. 3) If they approve, the application is submitted to his immediate boss —head of the factory, commune or army unit. 4) If he approves, it is forwarded to the Revolution in Education Committee of the Province, on which the university has a member. This committee judges the student on his record with his unit and decides whether he is politically knowledgeable and is regarded as a good revolutionary. 5) If the committee approves, it decides to what particular institution he will be directed. 6) The applicant goes to the designated university for an interview by college authorities; his educational level, literacy, etc. are checked, and he receives a physical exam. 7) If he is found physically fit and up to carrying on academically, he is admitted. All this in a government which keeps harping on the evils of bureaucracy. So the university has no real choice of students, it can only reject a candidate who does not meet the physical and academic requirements. And equally, the students have no choice of where they want to go or what they want to study.

I believe this is standard procedure for admittance to every Chinese university, and it illustrates the control of the government over students and teachers. Obviously it discourages, even prohibits, any independent thinking and discussion; there can be lots of talk but it must accord with what you have been taught, the line the government is taking; if you differ you are wrong, "in error," as they say, and must be helped and persuaded to change your mind and accept what is held to be right. This is very hard for westerners to accept, I know it is for me, I never could. But when I look at China and try to balance the gains for the masses of people with the prohibited intellectual and personal freedom of a now "silent minority," what do I see? I see a society in which every person is working as hard as he can at whatever

162

he does to "build up the country," to "serve the people." The spirit is extraordinary, as we keep saying. I don't believe it exists in any other country in the world. And yet I also see a society where as few as ½ of 1 percent has paid very dearly for the benefits to the others. As I have said so far, we have met no writers or artists, or people we refer to as "intellectuals." They must be in May 7th schools, and not the kind we visited. I don't know how to evaluate this. I don't know the statistics in the United States of who pays for the affluent society many of us enjoy. But it does seem as if the rich get richer and the poor get poorer as they increase in number, while here in China, no one is rich. And while many are poor by our standards, they have work, food, shelter and care, every one of them.

We were given a farewell dinner by our host, a man who is head of the Propaganda Department of the Revolutionary Committee of Hunan Province. He seems more of an intellectual than most of the other people we have met outside of the universities. Other guests were our interpreter and some of the local men who have been our companions here.

June 27

Peking

THIS MORNING about 9:45 we flew back here in a Viscount, a very comfortable and pleasant flight. But lunch was fairly revolting and I noticed that even some Chinese didn't eat much. It consisted of very brown cold chicken, sliced tomatoes and cucumbers (quite dry), black egg, slice of bread, two round cakes like pound cake, two square cakes just the same except with a sugary bottom, slice of watermelon and lichees, cool, watery apricot juice.

At the hotel before we left we found the medical group in all stages of travel sickness—vomiting, diarrhea, exhaustion, and the pregnant girl was the sickest of all. Unwisely, she has been eating a lot in this terrible heat, doing everything everyone else has done and to top it all off, she went swimming last night. Our interpreter, who is so sympathetic and helpful, got a Chinese doctor who prescribed something he promised would have no effect on her baby, would only make her feel better, but she refused to take it. She is a doctor herself and she makes me think of my mother who used to say that doctors' families were always sicker than anyone else's. In any case, she managed somehow to get to the airport and her group flew off just before we did. She looked so pale and sick and sat outside on the steps with an American friend and a Chinese nurse. The plane was some distance away and she walked slowly over to it in the broiling sun, the friend on one side and the Chinese nurse holding her arm. I wondered why all those big men in her group couldn't have carried her and why someone had not found her a hat or umbrella. I hope she hangs on to her baby but it would be a miracle if she does.

Also in the Changsha airport were many North Vietnamese, and two of their beautiful women. Perhaps they and the Cambodian women are among the most beautiful women in the world. Small, very feminine, thick hair beautifully done either up or back in a twist, and those becoming *odai's*, one of green flowered silk, the other in orange, worn over white silk trousers. Both women wore sandals with heels.

Arriving back here at the Chien Men hotel was almost like coming home. The people are all so friendly and our room was waiting, nice and cool as the windows had been shut. We have summer curtains instead of the heavy dark red velvet—fresh light yellow silk. We did some errands, picked up some seals we had had engraved and got my sandal fixed on the spot for the equivalent of two cents. After a marvelous supper (the food tasted delicious and familiar), we went to the huge stadium for an athletic show in honor of Madame Bandanarike, Prime Minister of Srilanka, formerly called Ceylon.

We were ready at 7:05 as the performance was scheduled to begin at 7:30. The stadium holds eighteen thousand people and it was already filled except for a long table reserved for the Premier and his guests, the grandstand section be-

165

hind it, some seats in the adjoining section next to us, and a few odd seats around us. Very soon these were filled with foreign guests including the Fairbanks, Lins, Han Suyin, her daughter and granddaughter (though some of these people are Chinese, they don't live here so are often treated as guests), Selig Harrison of the *Washington Post* who just came back from North Korea. He had expected to be there two weeks at the most but, as happened to H., the big interview with Premier Kim Il Sung kept being put off and put off. H. said he might still be there himself if he hadn't kept saying I was stranded in Peking and insisting that they let him leave.

Gradually the adjoining section filled up with the most spectacular ladies from Srilanka. Their saris were unbelievably beautiful and their long hair was done up in various classic ways, except for one medium-length bouffant which I didn't much like—it didn't go with her dress. There were quite a few children; especially appealing were three boys about eight to twelve, immaculately turned out in shirts and ties and short trousers. The men were dark and elegant. Not one of them wore jackets, just shirts and ties, which look much nicer and more comfortable and right for the climate than do our men's suits.

After they were seated our visiting congressmen, Gerald Ford and Hale Boggs (who disappeared in Alaska in October) and their wives, plus several Washington newspaper men and a NBC television crew, walked in behind them. By this time it was 8:45 and we had been sitting on our hard wood seats for one hour and twenty minutes. But we had to wait still longer and it was after nine when first one bell-like signal went off, followed in a few minutes by another. Soon afterward a spooky low, deep noise sounded, as if the devil were being announced, then the band struck up a rousing tune. In came a line of VIP's and interpreters with the Premier and Madame Bandanarike, and after a great deal of ac-

166

knowledging and waving, they sat down. No one bows here; actors accepting applause on the stage, athletes when they come forward to be introduced, simply step forward and stand for a few seconds. I never see anyone even bowing or nodding the way I find myself doing. I guess this is a break with that dreadful custom of prostrating oneself before a god or a king or a ruler.

The big shots sat at a dais table, with the interpreters sitting just behind them. English is spoken in Srilanka, dating from the days of British control, so the signs were in Chinese and English. The program was in both languages, as were the speeches and announcements. Madame Bandanarike had brought an elephant as a gift to the children of China from the children of Srilanka as it represents long life and is symbolic of their friendship. I expected an ordinary elephant to appear, but from the left, led by two men who towered above it, came a tiny baby elephant, no higher than a man's waist, with an orange brocade blanket embossed with stones that glittered like jewels, and its four ankles wrapped around with the same brocade. It was a marvelous sight. The men led the baby over in front of the guests while Madame made the presentation in English, which interpreters then translated into Chinese. A little Chinese girl accepted the gift in a businesslike official manner, first in Chinese, then she read her speech over again in English.

Finally the athletic program began, more than two hours after we had settled into our seats. I was astonished that anyone would expect eighteen thousand people to wait patiently for two hours while other people, no matter who they were, took their time over dinner and arrived when they felt like it, especially when a large part of the audience consisted of children who should have been home in bed rather than sitting there, red ribbons in their hair, waiting for the cues to wave their big red pompoms and shout out the ordered greeting. But no one seemed to mind, it is part of the Chinese way of life. The program was good, in fact excellent, gymnastics and exercises followed by fast badminton and Ping-Pong games.

June 28

THIS MORNING H. went to see Mr. Ma again and I went with Yao Wei to buy string and paper to wrap and mail by ship all the pamphlets and books H. has collected here and in Korea. Also I picked up our plane tickets to Shanghai for tomorrow.

Lunch with Chinese friends at the hotel. They tried to explain various aspects of the Cultural Revolution to us. I understand a little but I don't understand how, for instance, the faculties and administrations at most universities are the same as before the Cultural Revolution, that they have all been through the struggle, criticism and transformation, and they all have seen the errors of their past ways, and they all believe the present system is the only way. It seems too pat, too simple. I wonder if anyone really can change his point of view so completely, I can't help but be skeptical. What does come clear is that Mao and his faction realized that society was not evolving along the lines that they believe in, it was following the Russian, or revisionist line, as they say, which is not Mao's way, and thus he was losing control and power. They want their own kind of communism for China. So the young people, the Red Guards, were turned loose to stir things up, "to create revolution." Classes in schools and universities were suspended for as long as three and four years in some places. The Red Guards were allowed free transportation on all trains and they swarmed into the cities, through the villages, criticizing and denouncing people; they put up huge posters reading, for example, "I denounce Professor so and so, he says he is a revolutionary but he follows the line of Liu Shiao-shi. He is a revisionist." The professor was confronted by the young people, arguments ensued, heated discussions, fist fights and even armed violence. Finally the Red Guards split into two or more factions and fought among themselves. This is the period we in the West have heard most about; when the ultra left was strong, when the British Embassy in Peking was burned, the British correspondent, Anthony Grey of Reuters, kept in his house under intolerable conditions, not even allowed to read his own books, when there was ruthless damage of art objects and anything related to the past—fighting and torturing and killing in many instances. The Chinese are frank to admit that the situation was out of control, but by late 1970 sanity had returned to many areas, and while the Cultural Revolution is still going on in Tibet, for example, and other sections, they suggest it is not as anarchistic an upheaval as earlier.

We went shopping to buy a Chinese outfit for me, jacket, trousers, padded silk jacket and some real Chinese shoes. We found real Chinese stores in an old shopping street and each article was bought in a different store. The other shoppers in the stores couldn't believe their eyes: I was measured for each garment, and at one place as the saleswoman was

170

putting a tape measure around me Harrison said, "Turn around," and I nearly bumpled into a man's face as I complied. These people have never been taught by their mothers not to stare and not make someone feel conspicuous, or if they have their curiosity overcame their training. Closer to me than is polite stood a crowd of men and women, gaping, and pushing to get a better look. H. said he saw one woman's jaw actually drop, and until then he had never believed it could really happen. Everywhere we went we felt like the Pied Piper of Hamelin, followed by a staring, incredulous and increasing crowd. The cost of the things I bought, approximately, was:

Silk padded jacket	yuan 27.20	$12.00
Unlined cotton jacket	7.95	3.50
Unlined cotton pants	5.10	2.25
Fabric shoes	3.70	1.50
Cotton shirts	1.50	.75
	3.50	1.40

All about twenty dollars, which equals about two-thirds of the monthly pay of a well-paid industrial worker.

People can buy what they have money for with the exception of pure cotton, or anything made of pure cotton, including clothes. This is rationed (we were allowed to buy cotton articles without coupons as a polite gesture to visitors). But there is no limit on pure synthetics, cotton/synthetics, silk or wool. There is a good supply of all the ordinary consumer goods; necessities of daily life seem to be abundant. In all the stores we visited from the department stores in the big cities to the shops in the country communes, there was plenty of material by the yard, wool for knitting, ready-made clothes, shoes, underclothes, which consist of cotton knit shirts and union suits for men, and simple white cotton knit pants for women (very few brassieres, and those are not much like what the Maidenform girl dreams she goes dancing in). Detergents and all kinds of soap are plentiful, as are toothbrushes, toothpaste, and cold cream, the only cosmetic Chinese women use. Men use it too, especially in winter in the dry windy areas.

There are no kitchen gadgets as we know them, no electrical appliances. Cooking utensils are simple enamel, iron or aluminum pots, wood or metal spoons and forks. A Chinese friend in Hong Kong had asked me to bring her some long chopsticks, the kind she remembers from her childhood, being used in the kitchen, and although we looked in every store we visited, we never found any. But there were always large stocks of enamel basins, cups, pitchers, porcelain, usually very pretty; glasses, bowls, saucers, china spoons, teacups with covers, teapots.

Department stores, like ours, have sections for bedding— sheets, blankets, spreads, comforters; for stationery supplies —pens, pencils, typewriter ribbons, notebooks, etc., for books which are apt to be bound in red and about some aspect of the Revolution. Others are "how to" books of physics, engineering, building, mathematics. Radios, clocks, small kerosene stoves, foot-pedaled sewing machines, bicycles—all are sold under the same roof. The shops are always full of shoppers but whether they are really buying or "just looking" is very hard to determine.

On the way back from our shopping we stopped at the current exhibit of contemporary painting that is attracting so much attention here. In the entrance was one of the few huge white statues of Chairman Mao that we've seen. Throngs of Chinese swarmed through the halls, and it was hard to find enough space so we could get a good look at the pictures. The painting is meticulous, straightforward painting and the subjects were just what you would expect from art that must depict the life of the peasant, worker and soldier—peasants in the fields, soldiers marching, women in

172

uniform, fiery blast furnaces, dams, machines, Mao reading to and teaching groups that are clustered around him. I asked the meaning of a picture of a smiling girl with two adults; it represented a child, formerly deaf, just cured by acupuncture, telling her parents that she can hear for the first time. It was light and appealing compared to the more militant subjects. A few paintings had artistic and imaginative touches, but most were purely revolutionary, much the same as contemporary pictures I have seen in the Soviet Union, obviously the first step in art in a new, strictly ordered society. I would think even the most diehard believers and followers would become tired of this "art for and about the people" before too long. It is so representative and realistic that people may want something that reaches beyond their daily lives for inspiration and meaning. But at the moment there is no other meaning except the actual existence of the peasant, the worker, and the soldier.

This brings up a big question; how does a society that has come into being by and through revolution maintain its purity? How can it do what is known as "develop" and still be fresh and revolutionary? Some people I have talked to feel a revolution is necessary every few years to keep alive this feeling of dedication to ideals, the excitement in everyone working together for the good of *all* the people, for the country—and to prevent the inevitable bureaucracy.

Dinner with the Fairbanks, again at the Peking Hotel, and again, delicious. It is interesting to have their reaction to the things we have all seen and the many puzzlements we encounter. Of course, I am being very western; there really isn't any reason I should understand everything, or anything, Chinese or Asian. I should learn to accept without insisting on understanding—I should "Let a Hundred Flowers Blossom, Let a Hundred Schools of Thought Contend," as Mao once suggested.

June 29

Waiting at the Peking Airport
3:30 P.M.

WELL, THIS has not been our most interesting day. We got up at six and were ready to leave for Shanghai at seven. But at ten to seven we were told the plane was not leaving until one so we should leave the hotel at noon. We spent the morning waiting and reading and talking about what we have seen—and have not seen—the things we understand, the enigmas. It was very restful.

We came out here at noon and at ten to one were told the plane still had not come from Shanghai but we'd be leaving at three fifteen. Now the plane is in, but although it has been emptied of passengers and baggage, refueled and re-baggaged, we are still here. One good thing; everyone had forgotten about the pictures of our dinner with Chou En-lai and H. mentioned it to Yao Wei. Suddenly a few minutes ago, a man arrived with a set for us and one for the Dudmans. The pictures are very nice, an especially good one of H. meeting the Premier.

174

We have had lunch, H. and I, in the restaurant, good soup and real toast. I didn't feel very well this morning and it tasted just right. I thought of Mrs. Shapiro in Changsha who, when all of the medical group was suffering from some sort of sickness, said, "I'd give anything for a piece of toast." We were talking about different tastes in food and Yao Wei told us that a friend of his who went with the Ping-Pong team to the United States, had had a hard time with American food. He didn't really like it, and he couldn't get over the steaks, so terribly thick and "with blood running out of them."

The Vietnamese group that had been in Changsha were also lunching but they have departed. We watched some Chinese boys eating incredible quantities, each had one or two overflowing bowls of rice, a huge bowl of soup as big as those the hotel uses for several people, and mountains of greens and other dishes. I said to H., "No wonder they have so much night soil." I asked our interpreter if there is a way to ask for something by just saying please in Chinese, and then the thing I want, for instance, "Please, tea." He said no, you have to say the whole thing, "May I have some tea, please," or the person might think you wanted a special kind of tea, please tea, and wouldn't know where to find it.

Back at the Chien Men Hotel

We didn't go after all. Finally after four we took off and flew long enough to have some ice cream and immediately it was announced we were returning to Peking as the weather was bad in Shanghai. That seemed odd as they must have known about the weather before we started and it turned out there was something wrong with the radar, which could explain why the plane was delayed in getting here in the first place. Anyway, we are lucky to be here for the night instead of in the airport. We have our old room, 403, we have

175

had dinner, a bath, and I washed all my clothes. We hope to leave in the morning. It was a long fruitless day; five hours in the hotel, six at the airport and two in a taxi.

June 30

On plane to Shanghai

WE ARE actually flying and everything seems o.k. The flight takes two hours, which means we'll have the afternoon in Shanghai and perhaps it can be spent actually doing something rather than discussing what we want to do in the short time left to us. The same passengers who waited all day yesterday are on the flight, all Chinese except us and two large blond Frenchmen. A very sick man is lying on a stretcher in the back. He just had an operation, has some serious blood condition and is going to Shanghai where there are specialists in his illness. He was unconscious yesterday and looked terribly sick; this morning he is conscious and looks much better. Just before takeoff there was the usual announcement about smoking and seat belts, embellished by the following: "It is against the rules of our government to bring on board firearms, inflammables, poisons, explosives, radioactive and other dangerous materials. If you have any of these things with you, please turn them in to the stewardess

177

who will take proper care of them and return them to you
after you arrive at your destination."

June 30

Peace Hotel, Shanghai

AT THE airport we were met by the editor of the newspaper, a very pleasant man, and a not very friendly, unsmiling girl, who accompanied us to this hotel. Before Liberation it was called the Palace Hotel and it is nice and old-fashioned and on the river, though our room is on the side. However, that really is better because it isn't so noisy and we can see the river if we lean a little bit out the window. In the dining room on the eighth floor, one above our room, we have a table right next to the window and we watched the river traffic while we ate a fabulously delicious lunch. To me, nothing has been as good as the food in Wuhan, but here the vegetables are wonderful.

After lunch we had a tour of the city and went to the top of the building that used to be called Broadway Mansions because the street was Broadway in those days. Most of the foreign correspondents lived there and conveniently, the Press Club was on the roof. The view from there gave us an idea of how enormous the city is, one of the largest in the world. Shanghai looks much more European than Peking or any other Chinese city I have seen. Many of the buildings were put up by Europeans who were in business and banking here especially in the nineteenth and early twentieth centuries. From the roof the bridges across the Soo Creek remind me of Paris. Where the creek joins the Huang Pu River is the park that once had a sign advising visitors that "Dogs and Chinese are not allowed." Imagine if the Chinese had taken over an English city and put up a sign saying dogs and Englishmen not allowed; I don't see how they can ever forget such an insult.

The river is full of all kinds of boats, freighters, ferries, barges, long lines of sampans tied together creeping slowly up or down, pulled by a small tug. Much is produced here industrially for the home market and river transport seems to be increasing. The regular tugboats puff out the same thick black smoke we saw on the Yangtze at Wuhan.

Whenever I am in a city where the rivers are bustling with action, I wish our rivers had as much life. Just a few years ago in New York City where we have two wonderful big rivers, we had ferries, excursion and overnight boats up the Hudson, the night boats between New York and Boston, to Albany, to Virginia, and others; now we have only the Staten Island ferry, very few excursion boats and none of the overnight trips.

The women on the streets of Shanghai look smarter than those in other Chinese cities, their pants usually fit well and are more often black than washed-out blue or gray; many girls are very pretty, wear printed or colored blouses and their hair is more stylish, not just a bowl cut.

We visited the Municipal Childrens' Palace, housed in a mansion built by a rich English Jew, Mr. Kadorie. Though he had to leave China he still has large interests in Hong

Kong. The house is magnificent, and while it is all classrooms now, it has not been allowed to deteriorate like the landlord's house we saw; it is freshly painted and clean as a whistle, airy and cheerful. Many rooms open out of French doors to a balcony and all have big high windows. The spacious lawn is mowed and neat and the place looks kept up if not luxurious. It makes a wonderful place for the many activities of Childrens' Palace. Each district in the city has a childrens' palace, and the Municipal Palace gets its members from the others; it is a show place. Two days a week after school all children in the cities go to one of these establishments. They say it is voluntary but every child goes, and they say a child decides what he or she wants to do—music, painting, embroidery, boat models, or any of the many activities—but I believe his own school suggests what a child is now, or will be, best at, and that's what he does. How they arrive at this conclusion I have no idea. Once enrolled in piano, for instance, he doesn't change, and if one day he is tired of practicing and feels like joining the children in the painting class, he can't.

When we first arrived two little girls took H. by the hand, a boy and a girl took each of mine, and led us, first to see a few of the usual acts of singing and dancing, then from room to room, up and downstairs, to every classroom in the old capitalist's house. After that tour we watched target practice by a group of boys and girls lying down with their guns propped up as in guerrilla sniping and warfare—they were excellent shots, most of them hit the target. Next we were escorted through an obstacle course where H. bravely tried everything he could fit into or on without breaking it, crossing over water on a long swinging bridge, in and out of caves, hanging by his arms swinging from bar to bar. I was a sissy and only tried the swinging bridge, but later I tried my hand at Ping-Pong which H. didn't, and hit one hard ball

181

that my tiny excellent opponent could not get.

We must have watched every activity and we didn't see anything mediocre. Everything was excellent; two children aged five and six who had been taking piano lessons for a few months, played four hands for us, very nicely. A girl of about eight who has studied for eight months, played a theme from "The White Haired Girl" very competently. This music is simple and seems as if it is all in the same key, but nevertheless, the children are able and exact performers. We heard a group of violinists, seven to nine or ten; a roomful of accordianists, a choral group accompanied by an accordianist and professionally led by a girl no more than ten; several orchestral groups, all businesslike and efficient, but also looking as if they were enjoying themselves immensely. I only wish I didn't find it all so noisy. The voices seem especially strident and the music is belted out with more bangings and crashings coming from the huge red drums than anything I have ever heard, even here in China.

We watched a group of boys and girls making cut-out pictures, meticulous, minute and very pretty. The embroidery class does about the same work as is done in the factories. A group was making boat models, another making airplanes. The instructors told us that when these youngsters have made these complicated models they will know how to build any life-size boat or plane. Another group was learning codes and how to send and receive messages, other boys and girls were studying acupuncture and traditional herbal medicine. An older group was learning how to make spare parts for pumps, and they were turning out professional results in their workshop. Their teachers were workers from a nearby factory. This seems like an odd way for a child to spend the afternoon, not quite the same as playing the piano or learning to sew.

Every student in primary or middle schools in the cities all over China spends two afternoons a week in a Children's Palace doing something. I said to H. it was like an assembly line of disciplined conscientious energetic children, room 1 turning out pianists, room 2 violinists, room 3 dancers, room 4 accomplished embroiderers, room 5 what we would call Red Cross workers or nurses' aides, and so on. Like a factory —put in a child and get out an expert. When I think of the idle children on the streets and drugstore steps in our cities and towns, the contrast is staggering. These Chinese children are all learning to do one thing well, they have companionship of their own age which makes it fun, they have guidance from teachers, they are doing something constructive for themselves and because of that, for the society they live in.

In contrast to the American philosophy of life, there is never any emphasis on doing something for oneself, it is all for the good of the country, the party, the people. Mao has written about the dangers of individualism—it is an idea to be frowned upon. To me it is deadening and depressing to eliminate the individual, to adhere to one line of thought and action (though I think we go overboard the other way). In the palace drawing class, students were studying perspective. The illustrations looked like what we used to do in school, a series of boxes and angles. There is no such thing as free hand drawing, or painting anything you feel like, or portraying something the way it may appear to you even though it may look very different to others. The teacher draws an object on the blackboard and the student learns to copy it exactly. In the embroidery class, as in the embroidery factory, students learn to reproduce the same soldiers, peasants and workers; bridges, dams and smokestacks, plus the traditional animals and flowers that are the universal subjects of their art these days. No other subject matter, no artistic deviations are considered.

183

We were given the most fabulous dinner by Chu Yung-cha of the Municipal Revolutionary Committee Standing Committee, on top of the Park Hotel. I was thankful for our experience that has taught me to eat sparingly, especially at first, because invariably when I think there can't possibly be anything more, the best dish of all appears, and this keeps happening. In the beginning, you are tempted to eat too much of the first course, then the next, and so on. Then you find that each succeeding course is better than the last one, more appealing, more seductively served, and it becomes a problem not to offend your hosts. This dinner consisted of cold dishes served on a three-tiered lazy Susan in the middle of the table—meat platter, peppers and onion, peanuts, large shrimp slices. These were left on the bottom tier as the main dishes were brought in one at a time—large shrimp, liver and giblets fried crisp and very light; chicken in a hot sauce, brought to the table still in the transparent bag it was cooked in; bean curd and green beans, ravioli in crispy thin paperlike covering; fish, warm rice in broth (I hated this), a magnificent vegetable platter with two birds fashioned from white turnips, their wings of grated carrots, mushrooms, onions, amazing and delicious; junket; baskets cut from oranges filled with cut up fruit.

Before dinner Vietnam was the subject. They repeated what so many Chinese have said to us; the war must stop; until that day there can be no real relations with the United States.

July 1

THIS MORNING when I was doing my exercises I had the same experience as in Wuhan. Directly across from my window I saw a man doing his Chinese exercises with the same incredible concentration as the man I had watched there. But even though he didn't notice me, I felt the companionship of someone else doing what I was doing.

After breakfast we went with the Fairbanks to Fudan University, the largest and oldest in Shanghai, which has always been known for its educational institutions. At present there are twenty-four schools for higher education and several scientific research centers here. It was fun to be there together; two people from different professional backgrounds made for more varied questions and I felt we could have stayed on talking with the professors and administrators for hours more.

They described to us the status of scholars and teachers in pre-Liberation days, how exalted and special they had been,

185

how theoretical had been their approach to their subjects. Their pupils or the masses did not count for much. A lot of reference to the three divorces, from politics, people and reality. But, according to our hosts, professors now have become "tempered" by the Cultural Revolution and manual labor, have realized they had much to learn from the peasants, workers and soldiers as well as from students, and that they are now considered no different from anyone else.

We have heard all this before. John Fairbank, in his quiet way, said they might be interested to know that in the United States professors *were* just like anyone else, they had been downgraded for a long time. Moreover, students had a great deal to say about the universities and the courses. There was almost no reaction. Perhaps they just don't believe it, such a situation can't exist in a capitalist country; there is no point in talking about it. They are pure deadpan, either not interested, or don't care. In the past the Chinese felt contempt for any country but their own and maybe some of this feeling still lingers; they may also be too busy with their own affairs to care what happens in any other country.

One professor when teaching a contemporary novel would evidently take his students to a factory to see if the author had described his characters and their lives accurately. (I wonder what would happen to the author if he had not drawn his subjects realistically, and to the workers' satisfaction?) I asked whether they study the American Revolution as they study the French Revolution under the heading "Class Struggle in France during the French Revolution." The answer is that American history is incorporated into world history, lumped under capitalism and imperialism, not taught per se. I imagine our revolution is not recognized as a real revolution of the masses.

We visited the library where they are proud of their col-

186

lection of over a million books in many languages. I was amused to see in the English section devoted to scientific and scholarly sex studies, Havelock Ellis, etc., a copy of *Is Sex Necessary* by E.B. White and James Thurber. The books are there, but how much they are read is a question.

Almost immediately after lunch we were taken for an hour's boat ride on the Huang Pu River, up and down among the long lines of barges, junks, smaller flat-bottomed sailing boats so heavily laden they were nearly submerged with barrels, wood, coal, food; in and out among the freighters tied up on either side of the river or anchored in midstream. Most of the freighters were Chinese but we saw some from Norway, Greece, North Korea. The Chinese charter ships from other countries, as they haven't yet enough of their own to fill their needs. Our boat, like the one we took at Wuhan, was really a yacht with comfortable wicker chairs and tables in the bow and stern and a crew of at least six. With us were our interpreter, the three who have been with the Fairbanks on their whole trip, plus our Shanghai hosts and the Fairbanks' local hosts, making about fifteen in all. Things are done in a big way in Communist countries.

It was cool and refreshing out on the water and I wished we could have spent the afternoon that way, but the next event on our schedule was a visit to an industrial exhibition. I have become so weary of going to such things, and the word revolution is so planted in my mind, that I said to Wilma Fairbank, "I don't want to go to the industrial revolution." She and I decided against looking at turbines and motors and machines and went to the creative arts display. Most of the exhibits were of things we have seen in the factories and stores, but we also found lots of jade pieces in shades of green and lovely delicate pink, carved wood and ivory, boxes and trays inlaid with mother-of-pearl, needlepoint bags, artificial flowers, pictures and embroideries with revolutionary themes; reliefs with carved stones and some perfectly wonderful mechanical toys. These and the everyday blue and white china they make are my favorites.

The Fairbanks went off to a children's palace and we went to the hospital for severed limbs. I was relieved we didn't have to watch a real operation, or reconstruction. What we did see, the before and after pictures and the movies in color, were enough for me. The doctor in charge of this miraculous work struck me as the most aggressively dedicated to country and government of all the people we have met in China, praising Chairman Mao every other word and giving him most of the credit for these remarkable operations. The film showed cartoons of landlords and capitalists who, for example, cut off a worker's whole hand when some fingers had been only half severed. He then couldn't work any more and the capitalists wouldn't have to hire or pay him. Several instances of such inhumanity, then the new way of caring for these people and actually mending their arms and legs and hands and feet so that in a few months they could use them and work again. Strangely, he said he didn't remember talking to Tillman Durdin who was the first *New York Times* man to get into China last year and who interviewed him at that time in this same hospital. Tillman wrote in his article that after his China trip, he had talked to a doctor at the Massachusetts General Hospital in Boston about operations on severed limbs, and the cost of an operation for fingers and after-care came to $11,000—eleven thousand dollars! In China it is mostly free; all medical care is available to anyone who needs it and if he can't pay the small costs, it is taken care of by the government through communes and Street Committees and factories.

This doctor didn't mention anyone else as performing such operations, and when I asked him if he was in touch with doctors in any other countries, he replied that Chinese doctors read medical journals, of course, but they don't have a mutual exchange of ideas and methods with anyone. Mao preaches, "be self sufficient," yet they could without doubt learn what other medical men are doing, and they could usefully share with the rest of the world their own remarkable achievements.

We had dinner with the Fairbanks at our hotel and then, with our separate entourages and in our separate cars, we went to a vaudeville show, old-fashioned and, for the most part, awfully good, awfully funny, although I could now do some of the dances in my sleep. Wonderful acrobats and comedians! Best were two men who made noises like trains, animals, birds, babies, trucks, bombs and planes (not so funny), all with a perfect deadpan face. Deadpan Chinese is much more deadpan than American or any other kind of deadpan.

July 2

Canton

FINALLY, this morning in Shanghai, at the very last possible minute, we interviewed newspaper people at the newspaper office. We have been met and accompanied by several news-papermen but it has been difficult to get a picture of what they do and what, if anything, goes on in a newspaper of-fice. This was interesting; it more than made up for the un-pleasant scene at Wuhan where they were "too busy" to see H. Our host in Shanghai is chief editor of the paper, and he and many of the staff gave up part of their day off to tell us everything they could about the newspaper business in China today.

Our conference room was rectangular with big windows covering one whole side, Mao's picture at one end with a quotation in his special caligraphy, Marx, Engels, Lenin and Stalin in the usual order at the other end, and pictures of the famous Nanking bridge and Shao shan, Mao's birth place, along the fourth wall. We sat around a long table with the editors, and one girl who has recently been sent from some revolutionary committee, I suppose to keep her ears open as she seems to have no role on the paper.

The paper was founded in 1938 as a capitalist enterprise under reactionary rule; the purpose was to make money, the circulation between two and three thousand daily. After Liberation it was taken over by the government, reforms initiated, the building expanded, workers added, the total now being 740. It is composed of editorial, printing, press, administration, supplies and circulation departments. There is no advertising department as Chinese papers don't carry ads. Some of the editors are at May 7th schools at present, they go for three months at a time. While there they spend half the time on manual labor, the other half studying Mao's thoughts. Most people on this paper are city dwellers, knew nothing about the food they eat, how it grows, or about the life of the peasant. Now they respect his labor; they realize that many people would be unable to live without him.

Circulation is now nine hundred thousand for this four-page daily, two-thirds of which is outside Shanghai. It is read all over the country up as far as Peking. It reports the important events of China and the world, Shanghai news, Chinese propaganda, and Marxism and Leninism. Space is reserved for criticisms and reviews of new novels, plays, operas and films, such as "The Song of the Dragon River," and "On the Docks," for literary works by both recognized and amateur writers. Most of the articles seem to be written by amateurs for, as I have mentioned, we have not met a professional writer in all this time. Evidently they are all in May 7th schools, or else—where? One current author is a worker in a traditional pharmacy.

One regular column carries theoretical articles by revolutionary cadres. A story was written by a Party Committee of the sulphuric acid workshop of a chemical factory, for instance. It is quite usual for groups and committees to create things together, to make designs, paintings, write stories and poems. I think it is impossible for a true artist to function this way, but the Chinese say it is a good method of creating, that the finished work really represents collective thought.

The features submitted to this paper are revealing, for example "The Making of a Zipper," written by a budding author, describes a young apprentice in a zipper factory. He paid no attention to the quality of the zippers he turned out, just did a slipshod job. An old worker explained the importance of quality and took him to a department store where he sold zippers for a while. As customers told him that they preferred certain zippers because of their quality, he became aware of the importance of doing a job well. He went back to the factory, helped the old worker to make innovations and make an even better product.

"Innovations" is a prime word, always used to indicate how they have managed without outside help. After the Russians left in 1960, they "innovated," made do with what they had. Incidently, it is a very common practice for a factory worker to work for a while in a shop. He sees things from the other side, after which he can return to his factory with fresh knowledge of what people need and want. Consequently he may help devise a better product. The message of the story is a good example of combining theory with practice, of emphasizing that the only object in any labor is service to the people. The old workers, by their example, teach this philosophy to young apprentices. It's not so different from capitalist training in most businesses.

Other titles are "The Seed of Yenan," "Collecting Cinders," "The Sound of the Silent Needle under the Invisible Light," a story about acupuncture, and "Looking for Water," in which emphasis is put on investigation and innovation with wells, pumps and canals rather than through study and theory. The struggle in the countryside is a popular subject. These contributors to the paper are not paid; instead they are given souvenirs—literary works of Marx or Lenin, or posters.

The news agency of the Chinese government, *Hsinhua*, provides political comments and information, but this paper does its own background stories. For example, if diplomatic relations are initiated with another country, the paper researches and publishes material about that particular country. There is no news about the United States that is not related to Vietnam, and no comment on that subject from this paper, it is all from *Hsinhua*. They do have a correspondent in Japan but he has written only a few articles about sports, Ping-Pong and the delegates that go to Japan. He doesn't write about what the delegations do, however, and he never writes about internal politics or international affairs. We asked how people got their jobs and it seems the Ministry of Higher Education places them.

They were interested in Harrison's page, the "Op Ed" page in the *New York Times*. They asked him if he published anything by workers, meaning not professional writers, and were surprised when he answered that many of the articles are by ordinary people who just send them in, not professional at all. He also said that he printed all points of view, that he believes it is healthy to read and reflect on many different attitudes, even when you don't agree with them. The editor reacted to this with, "It must be very confusing for your readers to find so many different points of view. How do they know what to think?" This horrifies me; my idea is always to doubt and question, until you have thought about a subject from as many angles as possible. H. said that the *New York Times* editorials are considered liberal and that he considers himself a liberal. This was received

193

with polite giggles because "liberal" is a bad word according
to Chairman Mao, very bad.

On the drive out to the airport there are many different
kinds of trees and shrubs, plane trees, silk trees, lagustrum,
camphor trees, rhododendron, roses, cedars used as wind-
breaks, all mixed up together. On the approach to the airport and all around the building and the field are bright red
poster signs in English:

> "Countries want independence, nations want libera-
> tion, people want revolution, the triumph of our
> cause is inevitable."
> "We have friends all over the world."
> "Long live the great unity of the world."
> "Long live the unity of all the nationalities of
> China."
> "Workers of the world unite."
> "Unite to win still greater victories."
> "Serve the people of all the world."
> "Working people of all countries, unite."
> "Workers and oppressed of the world, unite."

Signs in Chinese preceded these on the road from the city to
the airport.

The flight to Canton is short, we were met and driven out
to our hotel, which is a new one on the river. It should be
very beautiful but it is stark and ugly and depressing. The
decor, or lack of it, is again like Mongolia and Russia, dreary
shiny varnished wood all through the building, unattractive
furniture, just no taste or sense of comfort or beauty. This is
so disappointing in China; I think even if they are communist and hate what the aristocrats had before and want to get
rid of everything capitalistic, they might have some sense of
how things look.

The smoke from the industrial chimneys across the Pearl
River is worse than any I have ever seen in my life any-

where, even in China. H. says some is from the chemical factories we can see on the far bank. Old trees line the walks beside the river on each side and from the hotel window it looks like a beautiful European city, then this terrible thick red-yellow smoke explodes out of the chimneys and hangs heavily over the whole other side of the river. The river itself is pretty and full of boats of varying sizes and shapes but no freighters.

As our official visit had ended in Shanghai, nothing had been arranged for us, no ballets, movies, vaudeville shows, or children's acts! No visits to communes or factories. And no one asked us what we wanted to do.

We walked along the bank under the cooling trees and even here where the people should be more used to foreigners than in the interior of China, we were stared at as if we were from the moon. In this city we see signs of a society that doesn't seem as controlled as in other cities; people looked messy and dirty, several men seemed to be preparing to sleep beside the river, and while there are no beggars, quite a few old men looked as if they had nothing, no job, no home, no money, and were just sitting on their haunches idly staring into space.

We had dinner by ourselves. The dining room in the hotel is upstairs so you have a lovely view over the rooftops or over the river if you can get a table near enough to a window. The atmosphere is rather like a second-rate commercial hotel compared to the friendly and more homey places we've stayed. The food is not as good as elsewhere and there are many unattractive heavy blond people eating.

July 3

Hong Kong

AFTER A noisy night and not much sleep, we took the train to the border, Shumchun. Here we went through the same simple courteous customs procedure as we had on entering China. We walked back across the bridge, leaving the red flags blowing in the hot wind, the pleasant-looking people in their dreary clothes, and the loud strident music we now know so well, and into the free world again.

196

Afterthoughts

A FEW DAYS after we got home from China I went to Bloomingdale's, my favorite store in New York, my home away from home, as Harrison says. There, for the first time since I had left for China in May, I suffered "culture shock." The store, as always, was crowded. But so are the stores in China. It wasn't the crowds of people that made the difference. It was everything else. On this sunny, warm summer day it just didn't seem like the old Bloomingdale's I knew and loved. But, of course, it wasn't really Bloomingdale's that had changed. It was I. I saw it all through eyes that had acquired—at least temporarily—Chinese lenses. Instead of the modest blue clothes of the Chinese, carefully concealing every contour of their figures, I found myself surrounded by girls in see-through tops, no bras, breasts of all shapes and sizes, jiggling and bouncing; skin-tight pants, skirts just reaching to the crotch. Older women seemed equally brazen in skirts showing legs that should not be seen, arms that

197

would be better veiled in sleeves, and so much makeup I was nearly blinded. Everyone was buying, buying, buying—things, things, things; not things they needed, not necessities, but the extras that have almost become necessities in our affluent way of life: belts, bags, chains, jewelry, blouses, dresses, pants, coats, sweaters, cosmetics—you name it.

I got used to it all after a while, but the initial shock at the contrast was stunning—far more pronounced than the contrast of Hong Kong to China. Perhaps because there we were still in the East, many people were still Chinese. Here every element was different.

Now I have been home long enough to type up my diary and to have a little time to think about our six weeks in China—time from a distance to try and evaluate what we heard and saw. I feel the way the Shanghai newspaperman thought H's readers must feel—I don't know what to think. There are too many aspects on each side, I don't know how to balance it all. In China so much is wonderful, exciting, inspiring, new in human experience: clean streets, no drugs, no dope, no crime as we know it, no venereal disease, no unemployment, no beggars, no starvation. Day and boarding nurseries for all children so mothers can work. Medical care for everyone, no matter if they can't pay for it. Simple but important jobs for old people so they feel a part of the community. Friendly places in the communes and villages for people who can't work. I saw nothing like our nursing homes with sad, forgotten people in bed or in rocking chairs, vacantly living out their endless lives. Somehow in China the old and incapacitated are absorbed into society, they are not freaks and outcasts.

While manual labor is overidealized, and some aspects seem absurd to us (the songs and dances about hog breeding), the Chinese recognize that to live by one's hands is not less important than living by one's wits. One is fundamental and necessary to the other. In fact, the peasant lives by both because he must have a wide knowledge to make his manual labor successful. I like this attitude. It can't help but produce a healthy-minded, appreciative society. The housewife who knows what it takes to make an iron; the secretary who realizes the hours it took to make her typewriter; the musician who sees how long the peasant works to get food; the government leader who shovels manure occasionally—all this makes for an appreciation of the whole and every person's part in it, not just one's special personal activity.

I wouldn't want to wear the same clothes as everyone else, even men, or wear the same pants and shirt whether I was taking care of pigs or going to see "The White Haired Girl" at a Peking theater. But there is something relaxing about such utter lack of fashion. While it eliminates variety, color and a certain amount of charm, it also eliminates the overemphasis on clothes and appearance that thrives in many countries in the West. And it furthers the feeling of equality. No one has more or better clothes than the next guy. The same is true of money and salaries. There is no struggle to keep up with the Joneses (or the Changs). Everyone has about the same.

But along with all the benefits to the masses go the restrictions on freedom as we know it. The Chinese have no freedom to talk, to argue, to disagree, even to think. No freedom to work at what they choose, to live where they want, to vote for their choice. Chinese cannot discuss and argue about their government if they happen to disagree with something—in fact, if they are young to middle-aged they will have been thoroughly indoctrinated since childhood and taught what to think. If they are older, they will have been "tempered" in the May 7th Schools. Chinese men and women work at what they are told and live where they are sent. It is true that now it is possible to try to change one's location if it separates husband and wife, but there are still many families living apart because of work. And there is never any question of having a voice, or a choice, in the government. All decisions are made at the top.

I wouldn't want to live like that. Because it is working now for China doesn't mean the same system would work for us. We are entirely different here in this country. While the uniformity of today's China gives it its strength, it seems to me that ours comes from our diversity. The United States is made up of different races, different religions and philosophies. People have different principles, different ideas. We recognize that what is good for one man may not be good for the next. We are an open, frank society and we expect our government to be honest and frank with us. The Chinese don't know what that means. They accept what their government says, believe it is the only truth, and never question.

Take, for example, the assassination of John Kennedy compared to the disappearance of Lin Piao. The United States government left no stone unturned in its effort to find the truth. It appointed the Warren Commission; there was the most thorough investigation and airing of all the facts, and the results were made public, on the air, in newspapers, in a book. Maybe some Americans were not satisfied with the results of the investigation, but they could not possibly argue that the government was hiding anything, or telling lies.

When Lin Piao disappeared, the Chinese government made no announcement. He simply was not there anymore. *One year later,* the government issued the news that Lin Piao had been plotting to overthrow Mao and seize power for himself, had tried to escape, and had died in a plane crash in Mongolia. No effort was made to put the details before the Chinese people. No reason was given for the year's delay in announcing that he had died. And I suppose that most of the Chinese people accepted these statements— didn't wonder or consider questioning anything.

I don't think Americans ever want to live like that, and as far as I could gather, the Chinese don't want to force their ways on other nations. Mao has made it clear that he hasn't got the answers for the world, has no secret recipe for American problems, says every society must find its own solutions.

But something has to happen here at home. Ways must be found to stop the drugs, the crime, the mugging and stealing. Somehow our national spirit must be lifted, we must become more brotherly and careful of each other. "Every man for himself" may not be the motto we can live by any longer in this complicated, shrinking world.

If there is one impression of China that, to me, remains stronger than any other, it is the spirit of the people, the strength of their unity, the power of their faith. I am reminded that Napoleon once said, "When China moves, she will move the world."

Travel Tips

ANYONE who has traveled a lot has her own special ideas about what is necessary to pack. While, obviously, the point in travel is to see and learn as much as possible, there is no reason not to be as comfortable as one can be without over-burdening oneself. Undoubtedly, more Americans will be going to China from now on, and I thought some of my ideas might be a help.

I never go away for a weekend without a hot water bottle, nail brush and a baby pillow. They can easily be squashed into any bag. And I never go on a real trip in my own, or any other country, without three folding plastic hangers and a stretchy line to hang things on in the bathroom. In the Soviet Union a rubber stopper for tubs and basins is necessary, but not in China. Though some of the bathrooms weren't very attractive, nothing was missing. But take your own washcloth. These are not supplied. Chinese toilet paper is crepey compared to ours, but o.k. However, as in all countries, you may be caught in a place where there isn't any. Carry a small package of tissues in your pocket or bag.

For the woman who likes pants, clothes are no problem in China. Two daytime pants, three interchangeable tops, and one outfit for evening are all you will ever need, no matter how long you stay. If you will be seeing people in the embassies, dining out a lot with foreigners, hobnobbing with other visitors, or if you are unhappy wearing the same thing every day and night, take more, or take a dress for a change, but you don't need to. Remember that all the Chinese, men and women, wear the same thing day after day, and at night. And if you do much traveling around the country, you will be thankful if you don't take too much. It is best to be able to carry your own bag. If it is heavy you may find a Chinese girl, much smaller than you, struggling with it, and that can be embarrassing. If you are unhappy in slacks, I suggest two medium-length skirts for day and a long one for evening with suitable tops. The first time I went to Asia I took a cotton suit with elbow length sleeves, sleeveless tops and a short narrow skirt. I learned my lesson quickly, had two skirts made in Delhi, one medium and one long, and hardly wore anything else the rest of the trip. Asian women dress to be comfortable and protected in their climate, so when it's hot, things are long to keep out heat and dust. In winter and cold, padded and lined layers are added.

Personally, I don't think it's appropriate to wear bare, short or tight and revealing clothes when native women dress modestly. I don't think we should copy other women, we should be ourselves. But it's more attractive not to be any more conspicuous than we are anyway. We should remember that this generation of Chinese hasn't seen many Americans and we should give a good impression of our country. Clinging wools and knits that we wear at home are not appropriate, neither are they comfortable for travel.

Something slightly loose is always better. By avoiding the extreme, a western woman can look smart and neat though simply dressed.

A raincoat and sweater are considered "musts" for travel in any country at any time of year, yet in the six weeks we were in China I wore neither. I wore what I call sneakers (Harrison calls them tennis shoes, but any light, fabric shoes with rubber soles would be the same) nearly every day, with socks, and Harrison was sorry he hadn't brought his. They are ideal for tramping around the communes and factories. Daytime sandals, for less strenuous sight-seeing, a dressier pair for evening, and the shoes I traveled in were all I took. If I went in winter I would take boots. Incidently, be careful of synthetics and man-made materials. With the exception of some forms of cotton/dacron or cotton/polyester, they make you sweaty and sticky in the heat, and don't keep you warm when it's cold, though some coats do keep out the wind. Once I took to Mongolia one of those quilted puffy raincoats that are advertised as ideal traveling coats for all weather. Every time I put it on it was like getting into a cold bed—I had to warm up the coat, it didn't do it for me. Real wool and cotton are best.

There is no risk of theft in hotels so you can take jewelry if you want to. I didn't take any except my wedding ring, a simple wristwatch and several identical pairs of inexpensive pearl earrings (because I lose one so often) which I wore at night when I felt like it. The clothes I took didn't require any jewelry, and as Chinese women don't wear any at all, I didn't bother. Some older Chinese women wear gold hoops in their pierced ears, but you never see anything on younger ones. However, very pretty rings and things are made now in China and you can buy them in the Friendship Shops, which are especially for foreigners. We also had a small traveling clock with an alarm, cameras, a shortwave radio and a typewriter, all of which we could leave anywhere—in airports, stations, or on top of our bags outside a hotel, without worrying that someone would take anything.

For any length trip I take three sets of underclothes and two nightgowns, and I prefer color or prints as they don't get grubby and gray looking. A wrapper that is presentable in a hotel room no matter who happens to come in is a necessity, and slippers. In China slippers are supplied on trains and in hotels, but it's nice to have your own.

I washed my clothes at night and they were dry in the morning. Hotel laundries are fast and good for men's clothes but are a bit hard on things. I took some detergent in tiny bags but found I could buy excellent washing powder in the hotel shop. I also took some individual shoe shine packets, and they came in very handy, especially for Harrison's shoes. Dry cleaning is available in all cities, takes about five days to a week—in hotels generally twenty-four hours.

I washed my own hair because I prefer to, and either slept with it rolled up or took some time in the morning to fix it. Most of the time I wore it twisted up under a scarf by day, and merely pulled back in a barrette at night, so it didn't need much "doing." But in the hotels in Peking there are adequate beauty shops for visitors.

The only things I would do differently if I had my trip to take over again would be to read more, to study as much about China as I could and to take only the bare essentials, with me, as I have listed.

A few Do's and Don'ts for visiting China:

Do as much homework as possible before you go. Read everything you can, past and present.

Do take a guide book. Nagel's is the best at present. It gives some past history and lists old sights and buildings that might be over looked.

Do always ask if it is all right to take pictures, especially in the vicinity of airports, stations, bridges.

Do take whatever you want to read as there are no newsstands in China, and no foreign magazines or novels.

Do take gin, whiskey, or whatever you prefer if you can't live without them, but they're heavy and a nuisance. Best get used to Chinese drinks.

Don't forget that you are a traveling exhibit of American culture. Most Chinese have not seen many (if any) Americans. You may form their ideas of us and our country.

Don't expect to be an independent tourist. Realize that while you may ask for anything, the Chinese will decide where you go and what you see.

Don't make a fuss if you can't see what you want. You'll only meet a blank wall. Remember you can't change the system.

Don't expect to be able to wander around freely in any Communist country. Sometimes you can, more often not.

Don't try to do too much. Rest when you can.

Don't eat too much until you are accustomed to the changes of food, drink, and weather.

Don't drink too much *mao tai*. It is stronger than you think, well over 130 proof.

Don't bother to take cigarettes. The Chinese have many brands, don't seem to be fearful of the dangers as we are, and many smoke like chimneys.

Don't be afraid to have your hair done in the beauty salons in the hotels.

List for Women—Summer

Two pair washable pants for day, or two skirts
   cotton/dacron is best, polyester gets heavy and hot, but it does keep its shape

Three tops to wear with above—washable
   I prefer tops that are worn outside. They are cooler and usually more becoming

Pants or long skirt for evening
One or two tops
   Take banlon or something synthetic as its bearable at night, washes and dries easily and doesn't wrinkle

Sweater
Raincoat
Wrapper
Slippers—terry cloth are ideal for hot places
Underclothes—your own preference
Nightgown—your own preference
Scarves for head and hair to cover and keep out wind and dust
   Two is plenty as you can buy pretty silk ones
Umbrella—optional as you can buy them, or parasols for sun, or big straw hats for about eighty cents

Shoes
   Sneakers, or simple comfortable fabric shoes with rubber soles for walking in communes, factories

Sandals for daytime when not so strenuous
Sandals or shoes for evening

Small bag in case you go on overnight trip and don't have to
take everything

Winter

Just about the same as above only heavier, warmer clothes

Wool pants suit and extra pants that can be worn with suit
jacket
Or suit and extra skirt that can be worn with suit jacket

Several tops
Two sweaters
Evening outfit, slacks or skirt and appropriate tops
Wool stole to go with above, and for use in day
Heavy weatherproof or storm coat
Wool hat or cap, gloves, scarves

Boots, warm and waterproof
Shoes for sight-seeing
Shoes for evening

Wool wrapper—the thin knitted kind, lined with silk, are
ideal for traveling. They are expensive, but last for
years and take up very little room
Slippers

For Men-Summer

Two pair washable pants
One lightweight suit—can be drip-dry
Shirts and sport shirts (remember the laundry comes back
the same day)
Sneakers or fabric, rubber-soled shoes

208

Two pair other shoes
Sandals—if you like them
Raincoat
Sweater
Underclothes, etc.—personal
Bathrobe and slippers, optional

Winter

Two suits
Two sweaters
Warm weather-proof coat
Hat or cap, scarves, gloves
Bathrobe and slippers
Underclothes, etc.—personal

Things you can buy in China

Toothbrushes and toothpaste
Shampoo
Shaving cream, etc.
Soap
Detergent
Socks
Sweaters
Sandals
Straw hats
Plastic raincoats
Umbrellas
Silk scarves

In the Friendship Stores for foreigners you can buy cosmetics, but they probably are not what you would prefer. However, they do sell:

Cold cream

Lipstick
Face powder
Talcum powder
We even saw some wigs for about $10

Be sure *to take:*

Aspirin
Kleenex
Absorbent cotton if you use it to remove cream, or apply lotion
Creme rinse for hair
Tampax
Any special medicine
Any special cosmetic
Washcloth
Pantyhose or nylon stockings
Prescription for glasses, or extra pair
Instant coffee or sanka. Hot-boiled water is always available, so is tea, but their coffee doesn't appeal to many Americans.
Film—you can buy only slow black and white, no color

Not necessary, but if you can, take a shortwave radio. When the country, the people, the language—everything is strange to you, there is nothing so comforting as the Voice of America or the nursery jingle that starts the BBC daily broadcasts.